Y0-BGT-612

A GIRL'S LIFE
IN VIRGINIA
BEFORE THE WAR

"AN EVENING PARTY."—*Page* 115.

A GIRL'S LIFE
IN VIRGINIA

BEFORE THE WAR

BY
Letitia M. Burwell

*WITH SIXTEEN FULL-PAGE
ILLUSTRATIONS BY*
William A. McCullough AND Jules Turcas

Harrisonburg, Virginia
SPRINKLE PUBLICATIONS
2001

SPRINKLE PUBLICATIONS
P.O. Box 1094
Harrisonburg, Virginia 22803

★

Originally published 1895.

FREDERICK A. STOKES COMPANY
NEW YORK

★

This reprint by Sprinkle Publications,
2001.

ISBN 1-59442-143-9

DEDICATION.

Dedicated to my nieces, who will find in English and American publications such expressions applied to their ancestors as: "cruel slave-owners"; "inhuman wretches"; "southern taskmasters"; "dealers in human souls," etc. From these they will naturally recoil with horror. My own life would have been embittered had I believed myself to be descended from such monsters; and that those who come after us may know the truth, I wish to leave a record of plantation life as it was. The truth may thus be preserved among a few, and merited praise may be awarded to noble men and virtuous women who have passed away.

L. M. B.

FOREWORD TO 2001 EDITION.

Do I know the true history of the Old South? My response must be given in the negative. Has an inheritance of hundreds of years of courage and devotion to principle been allowed to be buried in the pages of abolitionist history? A truthful reply must be given in the affirmative. Am I willing to stand by in silence when my ancestors are charged with perpetuating human slavery and for this purpose fighting to destroy the American Union? The reprinting of *A Girl's Life in Virginia Before the War* answers the last question with a forceful "No!"

Post modern historians, looking

FOREWORD

through their rosy tinted lenses of government education resemble the "blind leading the blind," and continue to bind us with the burden of guilt for slavery. Thomas Nelson Page in *The Old South,* 1892 prophetically spoke: "Before fifty years shall have passed, unless we look to it, the South's action will have gone into history as the defense of human slavery, and it will be deemed the world over to have been as great a crime against nature as the slave trade itself. How may this be avoided? By establishing the fact that it was not the South, but the time, which was responsible for slavery; and that this slavery with all its evils, and they were many, was the only civilizer that the African has yet known. By recording ere it be too late the true history of the South; by preserving and transmitting the real life of that civilization, so that future ages may know not what its enemies thought it to be, but what it in truth was."

FOREWORD

A reverence for the godliness and greatness of our past, portrayed in such men as Washington and Lee, and myriads of others whose names will never shine in the bright lights of this world, has convinced me of the importance of making known the truth from original documents such as diaries and journals, written not for monetary rewards but in order that future generations might know the truth from firsthand witnesses.

My reading of thousands of pages of journals and diaries led me back, by way of the beautiful Peaks of Otter, the same path taken by General Lee and his daughter when he visited the Burwells after the war, to my old hometown of Bedford, Virginia and to Avenel built in 1838 by the Burwells. It has been my privilege to become acquainted with this old southern family through the reading of *A Girl's Life in Virginia Before the War,* written by Letitia M. Burwell.

I have been once again impressed with

FOREWORD

the reality of the Christian religion on the opening page as Letitia described her birthplace and lot in life as being determined by God. The final pages conclude with the same refrain; "nothing happens by chance, and that our forefathers have done their duty in the place it had pleased God to call them." How refreshing to learn about the importance of duty as opposed to our post modern ideas about the importance of ourselves.

As we stand at the bar of history, being charged by those who have not personally witnessed our position, this book, along with many others of equal value, will testify in our defense for those things which were pure, honest, and of a good report in our southern culture. I, along with Letitia, trust that this volume may give us an increased desire to know and tell the truth, the whole truth, and nothing but the truth, so help us God!

Jacqueline Lee Sprinkle
April 2, 2001

LIST OF ILLUSTRATIONS.

	PAGE
"An evening party" . . . . *Frontispiece*	
"Carpenters always at work for the comfort of the plantation"	2
"Accompanied by one of these smiling 'indispensables'"	4
"I use to watch for de carriage" . . .	10
"I don't want be free no mo'" . . .	12
"She always returned in a cart" . . .	18
"Reading and repeating verses to him" . .	26
"My grandmother would show us the step of the minuet"	32
"There were old gentlemen visitors" . .	34
"Now, Marster, you done forgot all 'bout dat"	36
"Three women would clean up one chamber"	42
"Lunch by some cool, shady spring" . .	66
"His mission on earth seemed to be keeping the brightest silver urns"	78
"How dey does grow!"	86
"Where is my mutton?"	98
"Aunt Fanny 'spersed dat crowd'" . .	160

A GIRL'S LIFE IN VIRGINIA BEFORE THE WAR

CHAPTER I.

THAT my birthplace should have been a Virginia plantation, my lot in life cast on a Virginia plantation, my ancestors, for nine generations, owners of Virginia plantations, remain facts mysterious and inexplicable but to Him who determined the bounds of our habitations, and said: " Be still, and know that I am God."

Confined exclusively to a Virginia plantation during my earliest childhood, I believed the world one vast plantation bounded by negro quarters. Rows of white cabins with gardens attached; negro men in the fields; negro women sewing, knitting, spinning, weaving, housekeeping in the cabins; with negro children dancing, romping, singing, jumping, playing around the doors,—these formed the only pictures familiar to my childhood.

The master's residence—as the negroes called it, "the great house"—occupied a central position and was handsome and attractive, the overseer's being a plainer house about a mile from this.

Each cabin had as much pine furniture as the occupants desired, pine and oak being abundant, and carpenters always at work for the comfort of the plantation.

Bread, meat, milk, vegetables, fruit, and fuel were as plentiful as water in the springs near the cabin doors.

Among the negroes—one hundred—on our plantation, many had been taught different trades; and there were blacksmiths, carpenters, masons, millers, shoemakers, weavers, spinners, all working for themselves. No article of their handicraft ever being sold from the place, their industry resulted in nothing beyond feeding and clothing themselves.

My sister and myself, when very small children, were often carried to visit these cabins, on which occasions no young princesses could have received from admiring

"CARPENTERS ALWAYS AT WORK FOR THE COMFORT OF THE PLANTATION."—*Page 2.*

subjects more adulation. Presents were laid at our feet—not glittering gems, but eggs, chestnuts, popcorn, walnuts, melons, apples, sweet potatoes,—all their "cupboards" afforded,—with a generosity unbounded. This made us as happy as queens, and filled our hearts with kindness and gratitude to our dusky admirers.

Around the cabin doors the young negroes would quarrel as to who should be his or her mistress, some claiming me, and others my sister.

All were merry-hearted, and among them I never saw a discontented face. Their amusements were dancing to the music of the banjo, quilting-parties, opossum-hunting, and sometimes weddings and parties.

Many could read, and in almost every cabin was a Bible. In one was a prayer-book, kept by one of the men, a preacher, from which he read the marriage ceremony at the weddings. This man opened a night school—charging twenty-five cents a week—hoping to create some literary thirst in the rising generation, whose members, however, preferred their nightly frolics to the school, so it had few patrons.

Our house servants were numerous, polite, and well trained. My mother selected those most obliging in disposition and quickest at learning, who were brought to the house at ten or twelve years of age, and instructed in the branches of household employment.

These small servants were always dressed in the cleanest, whitest, long-sleeved aprons, with white or red turbans on their heads. No establishment being considered complete without a multiplicity of these, they might be seen constantly darting about on errands from the house to the kitchen and the cabins, upstairs and downstairs, being, indeed, omnipresent and indispensable.

It was the custom for a lady visitor to be accompanied to her room at night by one of these black, smiling "indispensables," who insisted so good-naturedly on performing all offices—combing her hair, pulling off her slippers, etc.—that one had not the heart to refuse, although it would have been sometimes more agreeable to be left alone.

The negroes were generally pleased at the appearance of visitors, from whom they were accustomed to receive some present on

"ACCOMPANIED BY ONE OF THESE SMILING 'INDISPENSABLES.'"—*Page* 4.

BEFORE THE WAR.

arriving or departing; the neglect of this rite being regarded as a breach of politeness.

The old negroes were quite patriarchal, loved to talk about "old times," and exacted great respect from the young negroes, and also from the younger members of the white family. We called the old men "Uncle," and the old women "Aunt,"—these being terms of respect.

The atmosphere of our own home was one of consideration and kindness. The mere recital of a tale of suffering would make my sister and myself weep with sorrow. And I believe the maltreatment of one of our servants—we had never heard the word "slave"—would have distressed us beyond endurance. We early learned that happiness consisted in dispensing it, and found no pleasure greater than saving our old dolls, toys, beads, bits of cake or candy, for the cabin children, whose delight at receiving them richly repaid us. If any of the older servants became displeased with us, we were miserable until we had restored the old smile by presenting some choice bit of sweetmeat to the offended one.

I remember that once, when my grandmother scolded nurse Kitty, saying: " Kitty, the butler tells me you disturb the breakfast cream every morning by dipping out milk to wash your face," I burst into tears, and thought it hard that, when there were so many cows, poor Kitty could not wash her face in milk. Kitty had been told that her dark skin would be improved by a milk bath, which she had not hesitated to dip every morning from the breakfast buckets.

At such establishments one easily acquired a habit of being waited upon, there being so many servants with so little to do. It was natural to ask for a drink of water when the water was right at hand, and to have things brought which you might easily have gotten yourself. But these domestics were so pleased at such errands, one felt no hesitation in requiring them. A young lady would ask black Nancy or Dolly to fan her, whereupon Nancy or Dolly would laugh good-naturedly, produce a large palm-leaf, and fall to fanning her young mistress vigorously, after which she would be rewarded with a bow of ribbon, some candy, or sweet cakes.

The negroes made pocket-money by

selling their own vegetables, poultry, eggs, etc.,—produced at the master's expense, of course. I often saw my mother take out her purse and pay them liberally for fowls, eggs, melons, sweet potatoes, brooms, shuck mats, and split baskets. The men made small crops of tobacco or potatoes for themselves on any piece of ground they chose to select.

My mother and grandmother were almost always talking over the wants of the negroes, —what medicine should be sent, whom they should visit, who needed new shoes, clothes, or blankets,—the principal object of their lives seeming to be in providing these comforts. The carriage was often ordered for them to ride around to the cabins to distribute light-bread, tea, and other necessaries among the sick. And besides employing the best doctor, my grandmother always saw that they received the best nursing and attention.

In this little plantation world of ours was one being—and only one—who inspired awe in every heart, being a special terror to small children. This was the queen of the kitchen, Aunt Christian, who reigned supreme. She wore the whitest cotton cap with the broadest of ruffles; she was very black and very portly; and her scepter was a good-sized stick, kept to chastise small dogs and children who invaded her territory. Her character, however, having been long established, she had not often occasion to use this weapon, as these enemies kept out of her way.

Her pride was great, "for," said she, "aint I bin—long fo' dis yer little marster whar is was born—bakin' de bes' loaf bread, an' bes' beat biscuit and rice waffles, all de time in my ole marster time? An' I bin manage my own affa'rs, an' I gwine manage my own affa'rs long is I got breff. Kase I 'members 'way back yonder in my mammy time fo' de folks come fum de King's Mill plantation nigh Williamsbu'g. All our black folks done belonks to de Burl fambly uver sence dey come fum Afiky. My granmammy 'member dem times when black folks lan' here stark naked, an' white folks hab to show 'em how to war close. But we all done come fum all dat now, an' I gwine manage my own affa'rs."

She was generally left to manage her " own

affa'rs," and, being a pattern of neatness and industry, her fame went abroad from Botetourt even unto the remotest ends of Mecklenburg County.

That this marvelous cooking was all the work of her own hands I am, in later years, inclined to doubt; as she kept several assistants—a boy to chop wood, beat biscuit, scour tables, lift off pots and ovens; one woman to make the pastry, and another to compound cakes and jellies. But her fame was great, her pride lofty, and I would not now pluck one laurel from her wreath.

This honest woman was appreciated by my mother, but we had no affinity for her in consequence of certain traditions on the plantation about her severity to children. Having no children of her own, a favorite orphan house-girl, whenever my mother went from home, was left to her care. This girl—now an elderly woman, and still our faithful and loved servant—says she remembers to this day her joy at my mother's return home, and her release from Aunt Christian. "I nuver will forgit," to use her own words, "how I use to watch for de carriage to bring miss home, an' how I watch up de road an' run clappin' my han's an' hollerin': ' Miss done come! an' I aint gwine stay wid Aunt Chrishun no longer!'"

Smiling faces always welcomed us home, as the carriage passed through the plantation, and on reaching the house we were received by the negroes about the yard with the liveliest demonstrations of pleasure.

"I USE TO WATCH FOR DE CARRIAGE."—*Page* 9.

CHAPTER II.

IT was a long time before it dawned upon my mind that there were places and people different from these. The plantations we visited seemed exactly like ours. The same hospitality was everywhere; the same kindliness existed between the white family and the blacks.

Confined exclusively to plantation scenes, the most trifling incidents impressed themselves indelibly upon me.

One day, while my mother was in the yard attending to the planting of some shrubbery, we saw approaching an old, feeble negro man, leaning upon his stick. His clothes were nearly worn out, and he was haggard and thin.

"Good-day, mistess," said he.

"Who are you?" asked my mother.

"Mistess, you don't know John whar use to belonks to Mars Edwin Burl—Mars Edwin, yo' husban' uncle, whar die on de ocean crossin' to Europe for he health. An' 'fo' he start he make he will an' sot me free, an' gie me money an' lan' near Petersbu'g, an' good house, too. But, mistess, I marry one free mulatto 'oman, an' she ruin me; she one widow 'oman, an' she was'e all my money tell I aint got nothin', an' I don't want be free no mo'. Please, mistess, take me on yo' plantation, an' don't let me be free. I done walk hund'ed mile to git yer. You know Mars Edwin think Miss Betsy gwine marry him, so he lef' her his lan' an' black folks. But we niggers knowed she done promis' twelve mo' gen'men to marry 'em. But she take de propity an' put on long black veil make like she grievin', an' dat's how de folks all git scattered, an' I aint got nowhar to go 'ceptin' hit's yer."

I wondered what was meant by being "free," and supposed from his appearance it must be some very dreadful and unfortunate condition of humanity. My mother heard him very kindly, and directed him to the kitchen, where "Aunt Christian" would give him plenty to eat.

Although there were already many old

"I DON'T WANT BE FREE NO MO."—*Page* 12.

negroes to be supported, who no longer considered themselves young enough to work, this old man was added to the number, and a cabin built for him. To the day of his death he expressed gratitude to my mother for taking care of him, and often entertained us with accounts of *his* "old marster times," which he said were the "grandes' of all."

By way of apology for certain knotty excrescences on his feet he used to say: "You see dese yer knots. Well, dey come fum my bein' a monsus proud young nigger, an' squeezin' my feet in de tightes' boots to drive my marster carriage 'bout Petersbu'g. I nuver was so happy as when I was drivin' my coach an' four, and crackin' de postilion over de head wid my whip."

These pleasant reminiscences were generally concluded with: "Ah! young misses, *you'll* nuver see sich times. No more postilions! No more coach an' four! And niggers drives *now* widout white gloves. Ah! no, young misses, *you'll* nuver see nothin'! *Nuver* in *your* time."

With these melancholy predictions would

he shake his head, and sigh that the days of glory had departed.

Each generation of blacks vied with the other in extolling the virtues of their particular mistress and master and "*their times*"; but, notwithstanding this mournful contrast between the past and present, their reminiscences had a certain charm. Often by their cabin firesides would we listen to the tales of the olden days about our forefathers, of whom they could tell much, having belonged to our family since the landing of the African fathers on the English slave ships, from which their ancestors had been bought by ours. Among these traditions none pleased us so much as that an unkind mistress or master had never been known among our ancestors, which we have always considered a cause for greater pride than the armorial bearings left on their tombstones.

We often listened with pleasure to the recollections of an old blind man—the former faithful attendant of our grandfather—whose mind was filled with vivid pictures of the past. He repeated verbatim conversations and speeches heard sixty years before—from Mr. Madison, Mr. Jefferson, Mr.

Clay, and other statesmen, his master's special friends.

"Yes," he used to say, " I stay wid your grandpa ten years in Congress, an' all de time he was secretary for President Jefferson. He nuver give me a cross word, an' I nuver saw your grandma de leas' out of temper nuther but once, an' dat was at a dinner party we give in Washington, when de French Minister said something disrespectful 'bout de United States."

Often did he tell us: "De greates' pleasure I 'spect in heaven is seein' my old marster." And sometimes: "I dreams 'bout my marster an' mistess when I'se asleep, an' talks wid 'em an' sees 'em so plain it makes me so happy I laughs out right loud."

This man was true and honest,—a good Christian. Important trusts had been confided to him. He frequently drove the carriage and horses to Washington and Baltimore,—a journey of two weeks,—and was sometimes sent to carry large sums of money to a distant county.

His wife, who had accompanied him in her youth to Washington, also entertained us with gossip about the people of that day, and could tell exactly the size and color of Mrs. Madison's slippers, how she was dressed on certain occasions, "what beautiful manners she had," how Mr. Jefferson received master and mistress when "we" drove up to Monticello, what room they occupied, etc.

Although my grandfather's death occurred thirty years before, the negroes still remembered it with sorrow; and one of them, speaking of it, said to me: "Ah, little mistess, 'twas a sorrowful day when de news come from Washington dat our good, kind marster was dead. A mighty wail went up from dis plantation, for we know'd we had los' our bes' friend."

The only negro on the place who did not evince an interest in the white family was a man ninety years old, who, forty years before, announced his intention of not working any longer,—although still strong and athletic,—because, he said, "the estate had done come down so he hadn't no heart to work no longer." He remembered, he said, "when thar was three an' four hund'ed black folks, but sence de British debt had to be paid over by his old marster, an' de

Macklenbu'g estate had to be sold, he hadn't had no heart to do nothin' sence." And "he hadn't seen no *real* fine white folks— what *he* called real fine white folks—sence he come from Macklenbu'g." All his interest in life having expired with an anterior generation, we were in his eyes but a poor set, and he refused to have anything to do with us. Not being compelled to work, he passed his life principally in the woods, and wore a rabbit-skin cap and a leather apron. Having lost interest in and connection with the white family, he gradually relapsed into a state of barbarism, refusing toward the end of his life to sleep in his bed, preferring a hard bench in his cabin, upon which he died.

Another very old man remembered something of his father, who had come from Africa; and when we asked him to tell us what he remembered of his father's narrations, would say:

"My daddy tell we chillun how he mammy liv' in hole in de groun' in Afiky, an' when a Englishmun come to buy him, she sell him fur a string o' beads. An' 'twas monsus hard when he fus' come here to war close; ev'y chance he git he pull off he close an' go naked, kase folks don't war no close in he country. When daddy git mad wid we chillun, mammy hide us, kase he kill us. Sometime he say he gwine sing he country, an' den he dance an' jump an' howl tell he skeer we chillun to deaf."

They spoke always of their forefathers as the "outlandish people."

On some plantations it was a custom to buy the wife when a negro preferred to marry on another estate. And in this way we became possessed of a famous termagant, who had married our grandfather's gardener, quarreled him to death in one year, and survived to quarrel forty years longer with the other negroes. She allowed no children about her cabin—not even a cat or dog could live with her. She had been offered her freedom, but refused to accept it. Several times she had been given away—once to her son, a free man, and to others with whom she fancied she might live—but, like the bad penny, was always returned to us. She always returned in a cart, seated on top of her wooden chest and surrounded by her goods and chattels. She was dressed in a

"SHE ALWAYS RETURNED IN A CART."—*Page* 18.

high hat with a long black plume standing straight up, gay cloth spencer, and short petticoat,—the costume of a hundred years ago. Although her return was a sore affliction to the plantation, my sister and myself found much amusement in witnessing it. The cold welcome she received seemed not to affect her spirits, but, re-establishing herself in her cabin, she quickly resumed the turbulent course of her career.

Finally one morning the news came that this woman, old Clara, was dead. Two women went to sweep her cabin and perform the last sad offices. They waited all day for the body to get cold. While sitting over the fire in the evening, one of them, happening to glance at a small mirror inserted in the wall near the bed, exclaimed: "Old Clara's laughing!" They went nearer, and there was a horrible grin on the face of the corpse! Old Clara sprang out of bed, exclaiming: "Git me some meat and bread. I'm most perish'd!"

"Ole 'oman, what you mean by foolin' us so?" asked the nurses.

"I jes' want see what you all gwine do wid my *things* when I *was* dade!" replied the old woman, whose "things" consisted of all sorts of old and curious spencers, hats, plumes, necklaces, caps, and dresses, collected during her various wanderings, and worn by a generation long past.

Among these old cabin legends we sometimes collected bits of romance, and were often told how, by the coquetry of a certain Richmond belle, we had lost a handsome fortune, which impressed me even then with the fatal consequences of coquetry.

This belle engaged herself to our great-uncle, a handsome and accomplished gentleman, who, to improve his health, went to Europe, but before embarking made his will, leaving her his estate and negroes. He died abroad, and the lady accepted his property, although she was known to have been engaged to twelve others at the same time! The story in Richmond ran that these twelve gentlemen—my grandfather among them—had a wine party, and toward the close of the evening some of them, becoming communicative, began taking each other out to tell a secret, when it was discovered they all had the same secret—each was engaged to Miss Betsy McC . . . This lady's name is still seen on fly leaves of old books in our library,—books used during her reign by students at William and Mary College,—showing that the young gentlemen, even at that venerable institution, sometimes allowed their classic thoughts to wander.

CHAPTER III.

As soon as my sister and myself had learned to read and cipher, we were inspired with a desire to teach the negroes who were about the house and kitchen; and my father promised to reward my sister with a handsome guitar if she would teach two boys—designed for mechanics—arithmetic.

Our regular system was every night to place chairs around the dining-table, ring a bell, and open school, she presiding at one end of the table and I at the other, each propped up on books to give us the necessary height and dignity for teachers.

Our school proved successful. The boys learned arithmetic, and the guitar was awarded. All who tried learned to read, and from that day we have never ceased to teach all who desired to learn.

Thus my early life was passed amid scenes cheerful and agreeable, nor did anyone seem to have any care except my mother. Her cares and responsibilities were great, with one hundred people continually upon her mind, who were constantly appealing to her in every strait, real or imaginary. But it had pleased God to place her here, and nobly did she perform the duties of her station. She often told us of her distress on realizing for the first time the responsibilities devolving upon the mistress of a large plantation, and the nights of sorrow and tears these thoughts had given her.

On her arrival at the plantation after her marriage, the negroes received her with lively demonstrations of joy, clapping their hands and shouting: "Thank God, we got a mistess!" some of them throwing themselves on the ground at her feet in their enthusiasm.

The plantation had been without a master or mistress for twelve years, my father, the sole heir, having been away at school and college. During this time the silver had been left in the house, and the servants had kept and used it, but *nothing had been stolen.*

The books, too, had been undisturbed in the library, except a few volumes of the poets, which had been carried to adorn some of the cabin shelves.

It was known by the negroes that their old master's will set them free and gave them a large body of land in the event of my father's death; and some of his college friends suggested that he might be killed while passing his vacations on his estate. But this only amused him, for he knew too well in what affection he was held by his negroes, and how each vied with the other in showing him attention, often spreading a dinner for him at their cabins when he returned from hunting or fishing.

I think I have written enough to show the mutual affection existing between the white and black races, and the abundant provision generally made for the wants of those whom God had mysteriously placed under our care.

The existence of extreme want and poverty had never entered my mind until one day my mother showed us some pictures entitled "London Labor and London Poor," when we asked her if she believed there were such poor people in the world, and she replied: "Yes, children, there are many in this world who have nowhere to sleep and nothing to eat."

Still we could not realize what she said, for we had never seen a beggar. But from that time it began to dawn upon us that all the world was not a plantation, with more than enough on it for people to eat. And when we were old enough to read and to compare our surroundings with what we learned about other countries, we found that our laboring population was more bountifully supplied than that of any other land. We read about " myriads of poor, starving creatures, with pinched faces and tattered garments," in far-off cities and countries. We read of hundreds who, from destitution and wretchedness, committed suicide. We read these things, but could not fully sympathize with such want and suffering ; for it is necessary to witness these in order to feel the fullest sympathy, and we had never seen anything of the kind on our own or our neighbors' plantations.

Our negroes' religious instruction, I found, had not been more neglected than among the lower classes in England, Ireland, France, and elsewhere. Every church—

there was one of some denomination near every plantation—had special seats reserved for the negroes. The minister always addressed a portion of his sermon particularly to them, and held service for them exclusively on Sabbath afternoons. Besides, they had their own ministers among themselves, and held night prayer-meetings in their cabins whenever they chose.

Many prayers ascended from earnest hearts for their conversion, and I knew no home at which some effort was not made for their religious instruction.

One of our friends—a Presbyterian minister and earnest Christian—devoted the greater part of his time to teaching and preaching to them, and many pious ministers throughout the State bestowed upon them time and labor.

I once attended a gay party where the young lady of the house, the center of attraction, hearing that one of the negroes was suddenly very ill, excused herself from the company, carried her prayer-book to the cabin, and passed the night by the bedside of the sick man, reading and repeating verses to him. I have also had young lady friends

"READING AND REPEATING VERSES TO HIM."—*Page* 26.

who declined attending a wedding or party when a favorite servant was ill.

On one occasion an English gentleman—a surgeon in the Royal Artillery—visiting at our house, accompanied us to a wedding, and, hearing that two young ladies had not attended on account of the illness of a negro servant, said to me: "This would not have occurred in England, and will scarcely be believed when I tell it on my return."

The same gentleman expressed astonishment at one of our neighbors sitting up all night to nurse one of his negroes who was ill. He was amused at the manner of our servants' identifying themselves with the master and his possessions, always speaking of "our horses," "our cows," "our crop," "our mill," "our blacksmith's shop," "our carriage," "our black folks," etc. He told us that he also observed a difference between our menials and those of his own country, in that, while here they were individualized, there they were known by the names of "Boots," "'Ostler," "Driver," "Footman," "Cook," "Waiter," "Scullion," etc. On our plantations the most insignificant stable-boy felt himself of some importance.

When I heard Mr. Dickens read scenes from "Nicholas Nickleby," the tone of voice in which he personated Smike sent a chill through me, for I had never before heard the human voice express such hopeless despair. Can there be in England, thought I, human beings afraid of the sound of their own voices?

There was a class of men in our State who made a business of buying negroes to sell again farther south. These we never met, and held in horror. But even they, when we reflect, could not have treated them with inhumanity; for what man would pay a thousand dollars for a piece of property, and fail to take the best possible care of it? The "traders" usually bought their negroes when an estate became involved, for the owners could not be induced to part with their negroes until the last extremity—when everything else had been seized by their creditors. Houses, lands,—everything went first before giving up the negroes; the owner preferring to impoverish himself in the effort to keep and provide for these,— which was unwise financially, and would not have been thought of by a mercenary people.

But it was hard to part with one's " own people," and to see them scattered. Still our debts had to be paid,—often security debts after the death of the owner, when all had to be sold. And who of us but can remember the tears of anguish caused by this, and scenes of sorrow to which we can never revert without the keenest grief? Yet, like all events in this checkered human life, even these sometimes turned out best for the negroes, when by this means they exchanged unpleasant for agreeable homes. Still it appeared to me a great evil, and often did I pray that God would make us a way of escape from it. But His ways are past finding out, and why He had been pleased to order it thus we shall never know.

Instances of harsh or cruel treatment were rare. I never heard of more than two or three individuals who were "hard" or unkind to their negroes, and these were ostracized from respectable society, their very names bringing reproach and blight upon their descendants.

We knew of but one instance of cruelty on our plantation, and that was when "Uncle Joe," the blacksmith, burned his nephew's face with a hot iron. The man carries the scar to this day, and in speaking of it always says: "Soon as my marster fin' out how Uncle Joe treated me, he wouldn't let me work no mo' in his shop."

CHAPTER IV.

THE extent of these estates precluding the possibility of near neighbors, their isolation would have been intolerable but for the custom of visiting which prevailed among us. Many houses were filled with visitors the greater part of the year, and these usually remained two or three weeks. Visiting tours were made in our private carriages, each family making at least one such tour a year. Nor was it necessary to announce these visits by message or letter, each house being considered always ready, and "entertaining company" being the occupation of the people. Sometimes two or three carriages might be descried in the evening coming up to the door through the Lombardy poplar avenue,—the usual approach to many old houses; whereupon ensued a lively flutter among small servants, who, becoming generally excited, speedily got them into their clean aprons, and ran to open gates and to remove parcels from carriages. Lady visitors were always accompanied by colored maids, although sure of finding a superfluity of these at each establishment. The mistress of the house always received her guests in the front porch, with a sincere and cordial greeting.

These visiting friends at my own home made an impression upon me that no time can efface. I almost see them now, those dear, gentle faces, my mother's early friends, and those delightful old ladies, in close bordered tarlatan caps, who used to come to see my grandmother. These last would sit round the fire, knitting and talking over their early memories: how they remembered the red coats of the British; how they had seen the Richmond theater burn down, with some of their family burned in it; how they used to wear such beautiful turbans of *crêpe lisse* to the Cartersville balls, and how they used to dance the minuet. At mention of this my grandmother would lay off her spectacles, put aside her knitting, rise with dignity,—she was very tall,—and show us the step of the minuet, gliding slowly and majestically around the room. Then she would say: "Ah, children, you will never see anything

"MY GRANDMOTHER WOULD SHOW US THE STEP OF
THE MINUET."—*Page* 32.

as graceful as the minuet. Such jumping around as *you* see would not have been regarded as dignified in *my* day!"

My mother's friends belonged to a later generation, and were types of women whom to have known I shall ever regard as a blessing and privilege. They combined intelligence with exquisite refinement; and their annual visits gave my mother the greatest happiness, which we soon learned to share and appreciate.

As I look upon these ladies as models for our sex through all time, I enumerate some of their charms:

Entire absence of pretense made them always attractive. Having no "parlor" or "company" manners to assume, they preserved at all times a gentle, natural, easy demeanor and conversation. They had not dipped into the sciences, attempted by some of our sex at the present day; but the study of Latin and French, with general reading in their mother tongue, rendered them intelligent companions for cultivated men. They also possessed the rare gift of reading well aloud, and wrote letters unsurpassed in penmanship and style.

Italian and German professors being rare in that day, their musical acquirements did not extend beyond the simplest piano accompaniments to old English and Scotch airs, which they sang in a sweet, natural voice, and which so enchanted the beaux of their time that the latter never afterward became reconciled to any higher order of music.

These model women also managed their household affairs admirably, and were uniformly kind to, but never familiar with, their servants. They kept ever before them the Bible as their constant guide and rule in life, and were surely, as nearly as possible, holy in thought, word, and deed. I have looked in vain for such women in other lands, but have failed to find them.

Then there were old gentlemen visitors, beaux of my grandmother's day, still wearing queues, wide-ruffled bosoms, short breeches, and knee buckles. These pronounced the *a* very broad, sat a long time over their wine at dinner, and carried in their pockets gold or silver snuffboxes presented by some distinguished individual at some remote period.

"THERE WERE OLD GENTLEMEN VISITORS."—*Page* 34.

Our visiting acquaintance extended from Botetourt County to Richmond, and among them were jolly old Virginia gentlemen and precise old Virginia gentlemen; eccentric old Virginia gentlemen and prosy old Virginia gentlemen; courtly old Virginia gentlemen and plain-mannered old Virginia gentlemen; charming old Virginia gentlemen and uninteresting old Virginia gentlemen. Many of them had graduated years and years ago at William and Mary College.

Then we had another set, of a later day,— those who graduated in the first graduating class at the University of Virginia when that institution was first established. These happened—all that we knew—to have belonged to the same class, and often amused us, without intending it, by reverting to that fact in these words:

"*That* was a remarkable class! Every man in that class made his mark in law, letters, or politics! Let me see: There was Toombs. There was Charles Mosby. There was Alexander Stuart. There was Burwell. There was R. M. T. Hunter,"—and so on, calling each by name except himself, knowing that the others never failed to do that!

Edgar Poe and Alexander Stephens of Georgia were also at the university with these gentlemen.

Although presenting an infinite variety of mind, manner, and temperament, all the gentlemen who visited us, young and old, possessed in common certain characteristics, one of which was a deference to ladies which made us feel that we had been put in the world especially to be waited upon by them. Their standard for woman was high. They seemed to regard her as some rare and costly statue set in a niche to be admired and never taken down.

Another peculiarity they had in common was a habit—which seemed irresistible—of tracing people back to the remotest generation, and appearing inconsolable if ever they failed to find out the pedigree of any given individual for at least four generations. This, however, was an innocent pastime, from which they seemed to derive much pleasure and satisfaction, and which should not be regarded, even in this advanced age, as a serious fault.

Among our various visitors was a kinsman—of whom I often heard, but whom I

"NOW, MARSTER, YOU DONE FORGOT ALL 'BOUT DAT."—*Page* 37.

do not recollect—a bachelor of eighty years, always accompanied by his negro servant as old as himself. Both had the same name, Louis, pronounced like the French, and this aged pair had been so long together they could not exist apart. Black Louis rarely left his master's side, assisting in the conversation if his master became perplexed or forgetful. When his master talked in the parlor, black Louis always planted his chair in the middle of the doorsill, every now and then correcting or reminding with: "Now, marster, dat warn't Colonel Taylor's horse dat won dat race dat day. You and me was dar." Or: "Now, marster, you done forgot all 'bout dat. Dat was in de year 1779, an' *dis* is de way it happened," etc., much to the amusement of the company assembled. All this was said, I am told, most respectfully, although the old negro in a manner *possessed* his master, having entire charge and command of him.

The negroes often felt great pride in "*our* white people," as they called their owners, and loved to brag about what "*our* white people" did and what "*our* white people" had.

On one occasion it became necessary for my sister and myself to ride a short distance in a public conveyance. A small colored boy, who helped in our dining room, had to get in the same stage. Two old gentlemen, strangers to us, sitting opposite, supposing we had fallen asleep when we closed our eyes to keep out the dust, commenced talking about us. Said one to the other: "Now, those children will spoil their Sunday bonnets." Whereupon our colored boy spoke up quickly: "Umph! *you* think *dem's my* mistesses' Sunday bonnets? Umph! you *jes' ought* to see what dey got up dar on top de stage in dar bandbox!" At this we both laughed, for the boy had never seen our "Sunday bonnets," nor did he know that we possessed any.

CHAPTER V.

ENGLISH books never fail to make honorable mention of a "roast of beef," "a leg of mutton," "a dish of potatoes," "a dish of tea," etc., while with us the abundance of such things gave them, we thought, not enough importance to be particularized. Still my reminiscences extend to these.

Every Virginia housewife knew how to compound all the various dishes in Mrs. Randolph's cookery book, and our tables were filled with every species of meat and vegetable to be found on a plantation, with every kind of cakes, jellies, and blanc-mange to be concocted out of eggs, butter, and cream, besides an endless catalogue of preserves, sweetmeats, pickles, and condiments. So that in the matter of good living, both as to abundance and the manner of serving, a Virginia plantation could not be excelled.

The first specialty being good loaf bread,

there was always a hot loaf for breakfast, hot corn bread for dinner, and a hot loaf for supper. Every house was famed for its loaf bread, and said a gentleman once to me: "Although at each place it is superb, yet each loaf differs from another loaf, preserving distinct characteristics which would enable me to distinguish, instantly, should there be a convention of loaves, the Oaklands loaf from the Greenfield loaf, and the Avenel loaf from the Rustic Lodge loaf."

And apropos of this gentleman, who, it is needless to add, was a celebrated connoisseur in this matter of loaf bread, it was a noticeable fact with our cook that whenever he came to our house, the bread in trying to do its best always did its worst!

Speaking of bread, another gentleman expressed his belief that at the last great day it will be found that more housewives will be punished on account of light-bread than anything else; for he knew some who were never out of temper except when the light-bread failed!

Time would fail me to dwell, as I should, upon the incomparable rice waffles, and beat biscuit, and muffins, and laplands, and marguerites, and flannel cakes, and French rolls, and velvet rolls, and lady's fingers constantly brought by relays of small servants, during breakfast, hot and hotter from the kitchen. Then the tea-waiters handed at night, with the beef tongue, the sliced ham, the grated cheese, the cold turkey, the dried venison, the loaf bread buttered hot, the batter-cakes, the crackers, the quince marmalade, the wafers,—all pass in review before me.

The first time I ever heard of a manner of living different from this was when it became important for my mother to make a visit to a great-aunt in Baltimore, and she went for the first time out of her native State; as neither she nor her mother had ever been out of Virginia. My mother was accompanied by her maid, Kitty, on this expedition, and when they returned both had many astounding things to relate. My grandmother threw up her hands in amazement on hearing that some of the first ladies in the city, who visited old aunt, confined the conversation of a morning call to the subject of the faults of their hired servants. "Is it possible?" exclaimed the old lady. "I never considered it well bred to mention servants or their faults in company."

Indeed, in our part of the world, a mistress became offended if the faults of her servants were alluded to, just as persons become displeased when the faults of their children are discussed.

Maid Kitty's account of this visit I will give, as well as I can remember, in her own words, as she described it to her fellow-servants: "You nuver see sich a way fur people to live! Folks goes to bed in Baltimore 'thout a single moufful in de house to eat. An' dey can't get nothin' neither 'thout dey gits up soon in de mornin' an' goes to market after it deyselves. Rain, hail, or shine, dey got to go. 'Twouldn't suit *our* white folks to live dat way! An' I wouldn't live dar not for nothin' in dis worl'. In dat fine three-story house dar aint but bar' two servants, an' dey has to do all de work. 'Twouldn't suit *me*, an' I wouldn't live dar not for nothin' in dis whole creation. I would git *dat* lonesome I couldn't stan' it. Bar' two servants! an'

"THREE WOMEN WOULD CLEAN UP ONE CHAMBER."—*Page* 43.

dey calls deyselves rich, too! An' dey cooks in de cellar. I know mistess couldn't stan' dat—smellin' everyt'ing out de kitchen all over de house. Umph! *dem* folks don't know nothin' *'tall* 'bout good livin', wid dar cold bread an' dar rusks!"

Maid Kitty spoke truly when she said she had never seen two women do all the housework. For at home often three women would clean up one chamber. One made the bed, while another swept the floor, and a third dusted and put the chairs straight. Labor was divided and subdivided; and I remember one woman whose sole employment seemed to be throwing open the blinds in the morning and rubbing the posts of my grandmother's high bedstead. This rubbing business was carried quite to excess. Every inch of mahogany was waxed and rubbed to the highest state of polish, as were also the floors, the brass fenders, irons, and candlesticks.

When I reflect upon the degree of comfort arrived at in our homes, I think we should have felt grateful to our ancestors; for, as Quincy has written: " In whatever mode of existence man finds himself, be it savage or civilized, he perceives that he is indebted for the greater part of his possessions to events over which he had no control; to individuals whose names, perhaps, never reached his ear; to sacrifices which he never shared. How few of all these blessings do we owe to our own power or prudence! How few on which we cannot discern the impress of a long past generation!" So we were indebted for our agreeable surroundings to the heroism and sacrifices of past generations, which not to venerate and eulogize betrays the want of a truly noble soul. For what courage, what patience, what perseverance, what long suffering, what Christian forbearance, must it have cost our great-grandmothers to civilize, Christianize, and elevate the naked, savage Africans to the condition of good cooks and respectable maids! They—our great-grandmothers—did not enjoy the blessed privilege even of turning their servants off when inefficient or disagreeable, but had to keep them through life. The only thing was to bear and forbear, and

>Be to their virtues very kind,
>Be to their faults a little blind.

If in heaven there be one seat higher than another, it must be reserved for those true Southern matrons, who performed conscientiously their part assigned them by God—civilizing and instructing this race.

I have searched missionary records of all ages, but find no results in Africa or elsewhere at all comparing with the grand work accomplished for the African race in our Southern homes.

Closing the last chapter of "Explorations in the Dark Continent," the thought came to me that it would be well if our African friends in America would set apart another anniversary to celebrate "the landing of their fathers on the shores of America," when they were bought and domiciled in American homes. This must have been God's own plan for helping them, although a severe ordeal for our ancestors.

In God's own time and way the shackles have been removed from this people, who are now sufficiently civilized to take an independent position in the great family of man.

However we may differ in the opinion, there is no greater compliment to Southern slave-owners than the idea prevailing in many places that the negro is already sufficiently elevated to hold the highest positions in the gift of our government.

I once met in traveling an English gentleman who asked me: " How can you bear those miserable black negroes about your houses and about your persons? To me they are horribly repulsive, and I would not endure one about me."

"Neither would they have been my choice," I replied. " But God sent them to us. I was born to this inheritance and could not avert it. What would you English have done," I asked, " if God had sent them to you?"

" Thrown them to the bottom of the sea!" he replied.

Fortunately for the poor negro this sentiment did not prevail among us. I believe God endowed our people with qualities peculiarly adapted to taking charge of this race, and that no other nation could have kept them. Our people did not demand as much work as in other countries is required of servants, and I think had more affection for them than is elsewhere felt for menials.

In this connection I remember an inci-

BEFORE THE WAR.

dent during the war which deserves to be recorded as showing the affection entertained for negro dependents.

When our soldiers were nearly starved, and only allowed daily a small handful of parched corn, the colonel of a Virginia regiment [*] by accident got some coffee, a small portion of which was daily distributed to each soldier. In the regiment was a cousin of mine,—a young man endowed with the noblest attributes God can give,—who, although famishing and needing it, denied himself his portion every day that he might bring it to his black mammy. He made a small bag in which he deposited and carefully saved it.

When he arrived at home on furlough, his mother wept to see his tattered clothes, his shoeless feet, and his starved appearance.

Soon producing the little bag of coffee, with a cheerful smile, he said: "See what I've saved to bring black mammy!"

"Oh! my son," said his mother, "you have needed it yourself. Why did you not use it?"

[*] Robert Logan, of Roanoke, Va.

"Well," he replied, " it has been so long since you all had any coffee, and I made out very well on water, when I thought how black mammy missed her coffee, and how glad she would be to get it."

CHAPTER VI.

THE antiquity of the furniture in our homes can scarcely be described, every article appearing to have been purchased during the reign of George III., since which period no new fixtures or household utensils seemed to have been bought.

The books in our libraries had been brought from England almost two hundred years before. In our own library there were Hogarth's pictures, in old worm-eaten frames; and among the literary curiosities, one of the earliest editions of Shakespeare (1685) containing under the author's picture the lines by Ben Jonson:

> " This Figure, that thou here seest put,
> It was for gentle Shakespeare cut;
> Wherein the Graver had a strife
> With Nature to outdo the Life:
> O, could he but have drawn his Wit
> As well in Brass, as he has hit
> His Face; the Print would then surpass
> All that was ever writ in Brass.
> But since he cannot, Reader, look
> Not on his Picture, but his Book."

This was a reprint of the first edition of Shakespeare's works, collected by John Heminge and Henry Condell, two of his friends in the company of comedians.

When a small child, the perusal of the "Arabian Nights" possessed me with the idea that their dazzling pictures were to be realized when we emerged from plantation life into the outside world, and the disappointment at not finding Richmond paved with gems and gold like those cities in Eastern story is remembered to the present time.

Brought up amid antiquities, the Virginia girl disturbed herself not about modern fashions, appearing happy in her mother's old silks and satins made over. She rejoiced in her grandmother's laces and in her brooch of untold dimensions, with a weeping willow and tombstone on it,—a constant reminder of the past,—which had descended from some remote ancestor.

She slept in a high bedstead—the bed of her ancestors; washed her face on an old-fashioned, spindle-legged washstand; mounted a high chair to arrange her hair before the old-fashioned mirror on the high bureau; climbed to the top of a high mantelpiece to take down the old-fashioned high candlesticks; climbed a pair of steps to get into the high-swung, old-fashioned carriage; perched her feet upon the top of a high brass fender if she wanted to get them warm; and, in short, had to perform so many gymnastics that she felt convinced her ancestors must have been a race of giants, or they could not have required such tall and inaccessible furniture.

An occasional visit to Richmond or Petersburg sometimes animated her with a desire for some style of dress less antique than her own, although she had as much admiration and attention as if she had just received her wardrobe from Paris.

Her social outlook might have been regarded as limited and circumscribed, her parents being unwilling that her acquaintance should extend beyond the descendants of their own old friends.

She had never any occasion to make what the world calls her "*début*," the constant flow of company at her father's house having rendered her assistance necessary in entertaining guests as soon as she could converse and be companionable, so that her manners were early formed, and she remembered not the time when it was anything but very easy and agreeable to be in the society of ladies and gentlemen.

. . . . .

In due time we were provided—my sister and myself—with the best instructors—a lady all the way from Bordeaux to teach French, and a German professor for German and music. The latter opened to us a new world of music. He was a fine linguist, a thorough musician, and a gentleman. He lived with us for five years, and remained our sincere and truly valued friend through life.

After some years we were thought to have arrived at "sufficient age of discretion" for a trip to New York City.

Fancy our feelings on arriving in that world of modern people and modern things! Fancy two young girls suddenly transported from the time of George III. to the largest hotel on Broadway in 1855!

All was as strange to us then as we are now to the Chinese. Never had we seen white servants before, and on being attended by them at first we felt a sort of embarrassment, but soon found they were accustomed to less consideration and more hard work than were our negro servants at home.

Everything and everybody seemed in a mad whirl—the "march of material progress," they told us. It seemed to us more the "perpetual motion of progress." Everybody said that if old-fogy Virginia did not make haste to join this march, she would be left "a wreck behind."

We found ourselves in the "advanced age": in the land of water-pipes and dumb-waiters; the land of enterprise and money, and, at the same time, of an economy amounting to parsimony.

The manners of the people were strange to us, and different from ours. The ladies seemed to have gone ahead of the men in the "march of progress," their manner being more pronounced. They did not hesitate to push about through crowds and public places.

Still we were young; and, dazzled with the gloss and glitter, we wondered why old Virginia couldn't join this march of progress, and have dumb-waiters, and elevators, and water-pipes, and gas-fixtures, and baby-jumpers, and washing-machines.

We asked a gentleman who was with us why old Virginia had not all these, and he replied: "Because, while the people here have been busy working for themselves, old-fogy Virginia has been working for negroes. All the money Virginia makes is spent in feeding and clothing negroes. "And," he continued, "these people in the North were shrewd enough years ago to sell all theirs to the South."

All was strange to us,—even the table-cloths on the tea and breakfast tables, instead of napkins under the plates, such as we had at home, and which always looked so pretty on the mahogany.

But the novelty having worn off after a while, we found out there was a good deal of imitation, after all, mixed up in everything. Things did not seem to have been "fixed up" to last as long as our old things at home, and we began to wonder if the "advanced age" really made the people any better, or more agreeable, or more hospitable, or more generous, or more brave, or more self-reliant, or more charitable, or more true, or more pious, than in "old-fogy Virginia."

There was one thing most curious to us in New York. No one seemed to do anything by himself or herself. No one had an individuality; all existed in "clubs" or "societies." They had many "isms" also, of which we had never heard, some of the people sitting up all night and going around all day talking about "manifestations," and "spirits," and "affinities," which they told us was "spiritualism."

All this impressed us slow, old-fashioned Virginians as a strangely upside-down, wrong-side-out condition of things.

Much of the conversation we heard was confined to asking questions of strangers, and discussing the best means of making money.

We were surprised, too, to hear of "plantation customs," said to exist among us, which were entirely new to us; and one of the magazines published in the city informed us that "dipping" was one of the characteristics of Southern women. What could the word "dipping" mean? we wondered, for we had never heard it before.

Upon inquiry we found that it meant "rubbing the teeth with snuff on a small stick"—a truly disgusting habit which could not have prevailed in Virginia, or we would have had some tradition of it at least, our acquaintance extending over the State, and our ancestors having settled there two hundred years ago.

A young gentleman from Virginia, bright and overflowing with fun,—also visiting New York,—coming into the parlor one day, threw himself on a sofa in a violent fit of laughter.

"What is the matter?" we asked.

"I am laughing," he replied, "at the absurd questions these people can ask. What do you think? A man asked me just now if we didn't keep bloodhounds in Virginia to chase negroes! I told him: Oh, yes, every plantation keeps several dozen! And we often have a tender boiled negro infant for breakfast!"

"Oh, how could you have told such a story?" we said.

"Well," said he, "you know we never saw a bloodhound in Virginia, and I do not expect there is one in the State; but these people delight in believing everything horrible about us, and I thought I might as well gratify them with something marvelous. So the next book published up here will have, I've no doubt, a chapter headed: 'Bloodhounds in Virginia and boiled negroes for breakfast!'"

While we were purchasing some trifles to bring home to some of our servants, a lady who had entertained us most kindly at her house on Fifth Avenue, expressing surprise, said: "*We* never think of bringing home presents to our help."

This was the first time we had ever heard, instead of "servant," the word "help," which seemed then, and still seems, misapplied. The dictionaries define "help" to mean aid, assistance, remedy, while "servant" means one who attends another and acts at his command. When a man pays another to "help" him, it implies he is to do part of the work himself, and is dishonest if he leaves the whole to be performed by his "help."

Among other discoveries during this visit we found how much more talent it requires to entertain company in the country than in the city. In the latter the guests and family form no "social circle round the blazing hearth" at night, but disperse far and wide, to be entertained at the concert, the opera, the theatre, or club; while in the country one depends entirely upon native intellect and conversational talent.

And, oh! the memory of our own fireside circles! The exquisite women, the men of giant intellect, eloquence, and wit, at sundry times assembled there! Could our andirons but utter speech, what would they not tell of mirth and song, eloquence and wit, whose flow made many an evening bright!

. . . . .

As all delights must have an end, the time came for us to leave these metropolitan scenes, and, bidding adieu forever to the land of "modern appliances" and stale bread, we returned to the land of "old ham and corn cakes," and were soon surrounded by friends who came to hear the marvels we had to relate.

How monotonous, how dull, prosy, inconvenient, everything seemed after our plunge into modern life!

We told old Virginia about all the enterprise we had seen, and how she was left far behind everybody and everything, urging her to join at once the "march of material progress."

But the Mother of States persisted in sitting contentedly over her old-fashioned wood fire with brass andirons, and, while thus musing, these words fell slowly and distinctly from her lips:

"They call me 'old fogy,' and tell me I must get out of my old ruts and come into the 'advanced age.' But I don't care about their 'advanced age,' their water-pipes and elevators. Give me the right sort of men and women—God-loving, God-serving men and women. Men brave, courteous, true; women sensible, gentle, and retiring.

"Have not my plantation homes furnished warriors, statesmen, and orators, acknowledged great by the world? I make it a rule to 'keep on hand' men equal to emergencies. Had I not Washington, Patrick Henry, Light-Horse Harry Lee, and others, ready for the first Revolution? and if there comes another,—which God forbid!—have I not plenty more just like them?"

Here she laughed with delight as she called over their names: "Robert Lee, Jackson, Joe Johnstone, Stuart, Early, Floyd, Preston, the Breckinridges, Scott, and others like them, brave and true as steel. Ha! ha! I know of what stuff to make men! And if my old 'ruts and grooves' produce men like these, should they be abandoned? Can any 'advanced age' produce better?

"Then there are my soldiers of the Cross. Do I not yearly send out a faithful band to be a 'shining light,' and spread the Gospel North, South, East, West, even into foreign lands? Is not the only Christian paper in Athens, Greece, the result of the love and labor of one of my soldiers?*

"And can I not send out men of science, as well as warriors, statesmen, and orators? There is Maury on the seas, showing the world what a man of science can do. If my 'old-fogy' system has produced men like these, must it be abandoned?"

Here the old Mother of States settled herself back in her chair, a smile of satisfaction

* Rev. G. W. Leyburn.

BEFORE THE WAR.

resting on her face, and she ceased to think of *change*.

. . . . .

Telling our mother of all the wonders and pleasures of New York, she said:

"You were so delighted I judge that you would like to sell out everything here and move there!"

"It would be delightful!" we exclaimed.

"But you would miss many pleasures you have in our present home."

"We would have no time to miss anything," said my sister, "in that whirl of excitement! But," she continued, "I believe one might as well try to move the Rocky Mountains to Fifth Avenue as an old Virginian! They have such a horror of selling out and moving."

"It is not so easy to sell out and move," replied our mother, "when you remember all the negroes we have to take care of and support."

"Yes, the negroes," we said, "are the weight continually pulling us down! Will the time *ever* come for us to be free of them?"

"They were placed here," replied our

mother, "by God, for us to take care of, and it does not seem that we can change it. When we emancipate them, it does not better their condition. Those left free and with good farms given them by their masters soon sink into poverty and wretchedness, and become a nuisance to the community. We see how miserable are Mr. Randolph's* negroes, who with their freedom received from their master a large section of the best land in Prince Edward County. My own grandfather also emancipated a large number, having first had them taught lucrative trades that they might support themselves, and giving them money and land. But they were not prosperous or happy. We have also tried sending them to Liberia. You know my old friend Mrs. L. emancipated all hers and sent them to Liberia; but she told me the other day that she was convinced it had been no kindness to them, for she continually receives letters begging assistance, and yearly supplies them with clothes and money."

So it seemed our way was surrounded by walls of circumstances too thick and

*John Randolph of Roanoke.

solid to be pulled down, and we said no more.

Some weeks after this conversation we had a visit from a friend—Dr. Bagby—who, having lived in New York, and hearing us express a wish to live there, said:

"What! exchange a home in old Virginia for one on Fifth Avenue? You don't know what you are talking about! It is not even called 'home' there, but '*house*,' where they turn into bed at midnight, eat stale-bread breakfasts, have brilliant parties—where several hundred people meet who don't care anything about each other. They have no soul life, but shut themselves up in themselves, live for themselves, and never have any social enjoyment like ours."

"But," we said, "could not our friends come to see us there as well as anywhere else?"

"No, indeed!" he answered. "Your hearts would soon be as cold and dead as a marble door-front. You wouldn't want to see anybody, and nobody would want to see you."

"You are complimentary, certainly!"

"I know all about it; and"—he continued—"I know you could not find on Fifth Avenue such women as your mother and grandmother, who never think of themselves, but are constantly planning and providing for others, making their homes comfortable and pleasant, and attending to the wants and welfare of so many negroes. And that is what the women all over the South are doing, and what the New York women cannot comprehend. How can anybody know, except ourselves, the personal sacrifices of our women?"

"Well," said my sister, "you need not be so severe and eloquent because we thought we should like to live in New York! If we should sell all we possess, we could never afford to live there. Besides, you know our mother would as soon think of selling her children as her servants."

"But," he replied, "I can't help talking, for I hear our people abused, and called indolent and self-indulgent, when I know they have valor and endurance enough. And I believe so much 'material progress' leaves no leisure for the highest development of heart and mind. Where the whole energy of a people is applied to making money, the souls of men become dwarfed."

" We do not feel," we said, " like abusing Northern people, in whose thrift and enterprise we found much to admire; and especially the self-reliance of their women, enabling them to take care of themselves and to travel from Maine to the Gulf without escort, while we find it impossible to travel a day's journey without a special protector."

"That is just what I don't like," said he, " to see a woman in a crowd of strangers and needing no 'special protector.'"

" This dependence upon your sex," we replied, "keeps you so vain."

" We should lose our gallantry altogether," said he, " if we found you could get along without us."

CHAPTER VII.

AFTER some months—ceasing to think and speak of New York—our lives glided back into the old channel, where the placid stream of life had many isles of simple pleasures.

In those days we were not whirled over the iron track in a crowded car, with dirty, shrieking children and repulsive-looking people. We were not jammed against rough people, eating ill-smelling things out of ill-looking baskets and satchels, and throwing the remains of pies and sausages over the cushioned seats.

Oh, no! our journeys were performed in venerable carriages, and our lunch was enjoyed by some cool, shady spring where we stopped in a shady forest at mid-day.

Our own ancient carriage my sister styled "the old ship of Zion," saying it had carried many thousands, and was likely to carry many more. And our driver we called the "Ancient Mariner." He presided on his

"LUNCH BY SOME COOL, SHADY SPRING."—*Page 66.*

seat—a lofty perch—in a very high hat and with great dignity. Having been driving the same carriage for nearly forty years—no driver being thought safe who had not been on the carriage box at least twenty years,—he regarded himself as an oracle, and, in consequence of his years and experience, kept us in much awe,—my sister and myself never daring to ask him to quicken or retard his pace or change the direction of his course, however much we desired it. We will ever remember this thraldom, and how we often wished one of the younger negroes could be allowed to take his place; but my grandmother said "it would wound his feelings, and, besides, be very unsafe" for us.

At every steep hill or bad place in the road it was an established custom to stop the carriage, unfold the high steps, and "let us out,"—as in pictures of the animals coming down out of the ark! This custom had always prevailed in my mother's family, and there was a tradition that my great-grandfather's horses, being habituated to stop for this purpose, refused to pull up certain hills, even when the carriage was empty, until the driver had dismounted and slammed the door, after which they moved off without further hesitation.

This custom of walking at intervals made a pleasant variety, and gave us an opportunity to enjoy fully the beautiful and picturesque scenery through which we were passing.

Those were the days of leisure and pleasure for travelers; and when we remember the charming summer jaunts annually made in this way, we almost regret the steam horse, which takes us now to the same places in a few hours.

We had two dear friends, Mary and Alice, who with their old carriages and drivers—the facsimiles of our own—frequently accompanied us in these expeditions; and no generals ever exercised more entire command over their armies than did these three black coachmen over us. I smile now to think of their ever being called our " slaves."

Yet, although they had this domineering spirit, they felt at the same time a certain pride in us, too.

On one occasion, when we were traveling

together, our friend Alice concluded to dismount from her carriage and ride a few miles with a gentleman of the party in a buggy. She had not gone far before the alarm was given that the buggy horse was running away, whereupon our black generalissimos instantly stopped the three carriages and anxiously watched the result. Old Uncle Edmund, Alice's coachman, stood up in his seat highly excited, and when his young mistress, with admirable presence of mind, seized the reins and stopped the horse, turning him into a by-road, he shouted at the top of his voice: "Dar, now! I always knowed Miss Alice was a young 'oman of de mos' amiable courage!"—and over this feat he continued to chuckle for the rest of the day.

The end of these pleasant journeys always brought us to some old plantation home, where we met a warm welcome not only from the white family, but from the servants who constituted part of the establishment.

One of the most charming places to which we made a yearly visit was Oaklands, a lovely spot embowered in vines and shade-trees.

The attractions of this home and family

brought so many visitors every summer, it was necessary to erect cottages about the grounds, although the house itself was quite large. And as the yard was usually filled with persons strolling about, or reading, or playing chess under the trees, it had every appearance, on first approach, of a small watering-place. The mistress of this establishment was a woman of rare attraction, possessing all the gentleness of her sex, with attributes of greatness enough for a hero. Tall and handsome, she looked a queen as she stood on the portico receiving her guests, and, by the first words of greeting, from her warm, true heart, charmed even strangers.

Without the least "variableness or shadow of turning," her excellences were a perfect continuity, and her deeds of charity a blessing to all in need within her reach. No undertaking seemed too great for her, and no details—affecting the comfort of her home, family, friends, or servants—too small for her supervision.

The church, a few miles distant, the object of her care and love, received at her hands constant and valuable aid, and its minister generally formed one of her family circle.

No wonder, then, that the home of such a woman should have been a favorite resort for all who had the privilege of knowing her. And no wonder that all who enjoyed her charming hospitality were spellbound, and loath to leave the spot where it was extended.

In addition to the qualities I have attempted to describe, this lady inherited from her father, General Breckinridge, an executive talent which enabled her to order and arrange her domestic affairs perfectly; so that from the delicious viands upon her table to the highly polished oak of the floors, all gave evidence of her superior management and the admirable training of her servants.

Nor were the hospitalities of this establishment dispensed to the gay and great alone: they were shared alike by the homeless and the friendless, and many a weary heart found sympathy and shelter there.

Oaklands was famous for many things: its fine light-bread, its cinnamon cakes, its beat biscuit, its fricasseed chicken, its butter and cream, its wine-sauces, its plum-puddings, its fine horses, its beautiful meadows, its sloping green hills, and last, but not least, its refined and agreeable society collected from every part of our own State, and often from others.

For an epicure no better place could have been desired. And this reminds me of a retired army officer, a *gourmet* of the first water, whom we often met there. His sole occupation was visiting his friends, and his only subjects of conversation were the best viands and the best manner of cooking them! When asked whether he remembered certain people at a certain place, he would reply: " Yes, I dined there ten years ago, and the turkey was very badly cooked— not quite done enough!" the turkey evidently having made a more lasting impression than the people.

This gentleman lost an eye at the battle of Chapultepec, having been among the first of our gallant men who scaled the walls. But a young girl of his acquaintance always said she knew it was not bravery so much as " curiosity, which led him to go peeping over the walls, first man!" This was a heartless speech, but everybody repeated it and laughed, for the colonel *was* a man of considerable "curiosity."

Like all old homes, Oaklands had its bright as well as its sorrowful days, its weddings and its funerals. Many yet remember the gay wedding of one there whose charms brought suitors by the score and won hearts by the dozen. The brilliant career of this young lady, her conquests and wonderful fascinations, behold! are they not all written upon the hearts and memories of divers rejected suitors who still survive?

And, apropos of weddings, an old-fashioned Virginia wedding was an event to be remembered. The preparations usually commenced some time before, with saving eggs, butter, chickens, etc.; after which ensued the liveliest egg-beating, butter-creaming, raisin-stoning, sugar-pounding, cake-icing, salad-chopping, cocoanut-grating, lemon-squeezing, egg-frothing, wafer-making, pastry-baking, jelly-straining, paper-cutting, silver-cleaning, floor-rubbing, dress-making, hair-curling, lace-washing, ruffle-crimping, tarlatan-smoothing, trunk-moving,—guests arriving, servants running, girls laughing!

Imagine all this going on simultaneously for several successive days and nights, and you have an idea of "preparations" for an old-fashioned Virginia wedding.

The guests generally arrived in private carriages a day or two before, and stayed often for a week after the affair, being accompanied by quite an army of negro servants, who enjoyed the festivities as much as their masters and mistresses.

A great many years ago, after such a wedding as I describe, a dark shadow fell upon Oaklands.

The eldest daughter, young and beautiful, soon to marry a gentleman* of high character, charming manners, and large estate, one night, while the preparations were in progress for her nuptials, saw in a vision vivid pictures of what would befall her if she married. The vision showed her: a gay wedding, herself the bride; the marriage jaunt to her husband's home in a distant county; the incidents of the journey; her arrival at her new home; her sickness and

* Colonel Tom Preston.

death; the funeral procession back to Oaklands; the open grave; the bearers of her bier—those who a few weeks before had danced at the wedding; herself a corpse in her bridal dress; her newly turfed grave with a bird singing in the tree above.

This vision produced such an impression that she awakened her sister and told her of it.

For three successive nights the vision appeared, which so affected her spirits that she determined not to marry. But after some months, persuaded by her family to think no more of the dream which continually haunted her, she allowed the marriage to take place.

All was a realization of the vision: the wedding, the journey to her new home,—every incident, however small, had been presented before her in the dream.

As the bridal party approached the house of an old lady near Abingdon, who had made preparations for their entertainment, servants were hurrying to and fro in great excitement, and one was galloping off for a doctor, as the old lady had been suddenly seized with a violent illness. Even this was another picture in the ill-omened vision of the bride, who every day found something occurring to remind her of it, until in six months her own death made the last sad scene of her dream. And the funeral procession back to Oaklands, the persons officiating, the grave,—all proved a realization of her vision.

After this her husband, a man of true Christian character, sought in foreign lands to disperse the gloom overshadowing his life. But whether on the summit of Mount Blanc or the lava-crusted Vesuvius; among the classic hills of Rome or the palaces of France; in the art-galleries of Italy or the regions of the Holy Land,—he carries ever in his heart the image of his fair bride and the quiet grave at Oaklands.

CHAPTER VIII.

ANOTHER charming residence, not far from Oaklands,* which attracted visitors from various quarters, was Buena Vista, where we passed many happy hours of childhood.

This residence—large and handsome—was situated on an eminence overlooking pastures and sunny slopes, with forests and mountain views in the distance.

The interior of the house accorded with the outside, every article being elegant and substantial.

The owner,† a gentleman of polished manners, kind and generous disposition, a sincere Christian and zealous churchman, was honored and beloved by all who knew him.

His daughters, a band of lovely young girls, presided over his house, dispensing its hospitality with grace and dignity. Their mother's death, which occurred when they

---

* General Watts's place, Roanoke.
† George P. Tayloe, Esq.

were very young, had given them household cares which would have been considerable but for the assistance of Uncle Billy, the butler,—an all-important character presiding with imposing dignity over domestic affairs.

His jet-black face was relieved by a head of gray hair with a small, round, bald centerpiece; and the expression of his face was calm and serene as he presided over the pantry, the table, and the tea-waiters.

His mission on earth seemed to be keeping the brightest silver urns, sugar-dishes, cream-jugs, and spoons; flavoring the best ice-creams; buttering the hottest rolls, muffins, and waffles; chopping the best salads; folding the whitest napkins; handing the best tea and cakes in the parlor in the evenings; and cooling the best wine for dinner. Indeed, he was so essentially a part of the establishment that in recalling those old days at Buena Vista the form of Uncle Billy comes silently back from the past and takes its old place about the parlors, the halls, and the dining-room, making the picture complete.

And thus upon the canvas of every old

"HIS MISSION ON EARTH SEEMED TO BE KEEPING THE BRIGHTEST
SILVER URNS."—*Page 78.*

home picture come to their accustomed places the forms of dusky friends, who once shared our homes, our firesides, our affections,—and who will share them, as in the past, never more.

. . . . .

Of all the plantation homes we loved and visited, the brightest, sweetest memories cluster around Grove Hill,* a grand old place in the midst of scenery lovely and picturesque, to reach which we made a journey across the Blue Ridge—those giant mountains from whose winding roads and lofty heights we had glimpses of exquisite scenery in the valleys below.

Thus winding slowly around these mountain heights and peeping down from our old carriage windows, we beheld nature in its wildest luxuriance. The deep solitude ; the glowing sunlight over rock, forest, and glen ; the green valleys deep down beneath, diversified by alternate light and shadow,—all together photographed on our hearts pictures never to fade.

Not all the towers, minarets, obelisks, palaces, gem-studded domes of " art and man's

* The old seat of the Breckinridges, Botetourt County.

device," can reach the soul like one of these sun-tinted pictures in their convex frames of rock and vines!

Arrived at Grove Hill, how enthusiastic the welcome from each member of the family assembled in the front porch to meet us! How joyous the laugh! How deliciously cool the wide halls, the spacious parlor, the dark polished walnut floors! How bright the flowers! How gay the spirits of all assembled!

One was sure of meeting here pleasant people from Virginia, Baltimore, Florida, South Carolina, and Kentucky, with whom the house was filled from May till November.

How delightfully passed the days, the weeks! What merry excursions, fishing-parties, riding-parties to the Indian Spring, the Cave, the Natural Bridge! What pleasant music, and tableaux, and dancing, in the evenings!

For the tableaux we had only to open an old chest in the garret and help ourselves to rich embroidered white and scarlet dresses, with other costumes worn by the grandmother of the family nearly a hundred years before, when her husband was in public life and she one of the queens of society.

What sprightly *conversazioni* in our rooms at night!—young girls *will* become confidential and eloquent with each other at night, however reserved and quiet during the day.

Late in the night these talks continued, with puns and laughter, until checked by a certain young gentleman, now a minister, who was wont to bring out his flute in the flower-garden under our windows, and give himself up for an hour or more to the most sentimental and touching strains, thus breaking in upon sprightly remarks and repartees, some of which are remembered to this day. A characteristic conversation ran thus:

"Girls!" said one, "would it not be charming if we could all take a trip together to Niagara?"

"Well, why could we not?" was the response.

"Oh!" replied another, "the idea of us poor Virginia girls taking a trip!"

"Indeed," said one of the Grove Hill girls, "it would be impossible. For here are we on this immense estate,—four thousand acres, two large, handsome residences, and three hundred negroes,—regarded as wealthy, and yet, to save our lives, we could not raise money enough for a trip to New York!"

"Nor get a silk-velvet cloak!" said her sister, laughing.

"Yes," replied the other. "Girls! I have been longing and longing for a silk-velvet cloak, but never could get the money to buy one. But last Sunday, at the village church, what should I see but one of the Joneses sweeping in with a long velvet cloak almost touching the floor! And you could set her father's house in our back hall! But, then, she is so fortunate as to own no negroes."

"What a happy girl she must be!" cried a chorus of voices. "No negroes to support! We could go to New York and Niagara, and have velvet cloaks, too, if we only had no negroes to support! But all *our* money goes to provide for them as soon as the crops are sold!"

"Yes," said one of the Grove Hill girls; "here is our large house without an article of modern furniture. The parlor curtains are one hundred years old, the old-fashioned mirrors and recess tables one hundred years old, and we long in vain for money to buy something new."

"Well!" said one of the sprightliest girls, "we can get up some of our old diamond rings or breastpins which some of us have inherited, and travel on appearances! We have no modern clothes, but the old rings will make us look rich! And a party of *poor, rich Virginians* will attract the commiseration and consideration of the world when it is known that for generations we have not been able to leave our plantations!"

After these conversations we would fall asleep, and sleep profoundly, until aroused next morning by an army of servants polishing the hall floors, waxing and rubbing them with a long-handled brush weighted by an oven lid. This made the floor like a "sea of glass," and dangerous to walk upon immediately after the polishing process, being especially disastrous to small children, who were continually slipping and falling before breakfast.

The lady[*] presiding over this establish-

[*] Mrs. Cary Breckinridge.

ment possessed a cultivated mind, bright conversational powers, and gentle temper, with a force of character which enabled her judiciously to direct the affairs of her household, as well as the training and education of her children.

She always employed an accomplished tutor, who added to the attractiveness of her home circle.

She helped the boys with their Latin, and the girls with their compositions. In her quiet way she governed, controlled, suggested everything; so that her presence was required everywhere at once.

While in the parlor entertaining her guests with bright, agreeable conversation, she was sure to be wanted by the cooks (there were six!) to "taste or flavor" something in the kitchen; or by the gardener, to direct the planting of certain seeds or roots,—and so with every department. Even the minister —there was always one living in her house —would call her out to consult over his text and sermon for the next Sunday, saying he could rely upon her judgment and discrimination.

Never thinking of herself, her heart overflowing with sympathy and interest for others, she entered into the pleasures of the young as well as the sorrows of the old.

If the boys came in from a fox or deer chase, their pleasure was incomplete until it had been described to her and enjoyed with her again.

The flower-vases were never entirely beautiful until her hand had helped to arrange the flowers.

The girls' laces were never perfect until she had gathered and crimped them.

Her sons were never so happy as when holding her hand and caressing her. And the summer twilight found her always in the vine-covered porch, seated by her husband,—a dear, kind old gentleman,—her hand resting in his, while he quietly and happily smoked his pipe after the day's riding over his plantation, interviewing overseers, millers, and blacksmiths, and settling up accounts.

One more reminiscence, and the Grove Hill picture will be done. No Virginia home being complete without some prominent negro character, the picture lacking this would be untrue to nature, and without the finishing touch. And not to have "stepped in" to pay our respects to old Aunt Betsy during a visit to Grove Hill would have been looked upon—as it should be to omit it here—a great breach of civility; for the old woman always received us at her door with a cordial welcome and a hearty shake of the hand.

"Lor' bless de child'en!" she would say. "How dey does grow! Done grown up young ladies! Set down, honey. I mighty glad to see you. An' why didn't your ma* come? I would love to see Miss Fanny. She always was so good an' so pretty. Seems to me it aint been no time sence she and Miss Emma"—her own mistress—"use' to play dolls togedder, an' I use' to bake sweet cakes for dem, an' cut dem out wid de pepper-box top for dar doll parties; an' dey loved each other like sisters."

"Well, Aunt Betsy," we would ask, "how is your rheumatism now?"

"Lor', honey, I nuver spec's to git over dat. But some days I can hobble out an' feed de chickens; an' I can set at my window an' make the black child'en feed 'em, an' I love to think I'm some 'count to Miss

* " Miss Fanny."

"HOW DEY DOES GROW!"—*Page* 86.

Emma. An' Miss Emma's child'en can't do 'thout old 'Mammy Betsy,' for I takes care of all dar pet chickens. Me an' my ole man gittin' mighty ole now; but Miss Emma an' all her child'en so good to us we has pleasure in livin' yet."

At last the shadows began to fall dark and chill upon this once bright and happy home.

Old Aunt Betsy lived to see the four boys —her mistress's brave and noble sons— buckle their armor on and go forth to battle for the home they loved so well,—the youngest still so young that he loved his pet chickens, which were left to "Mammy Betsy's" special care ; and when the sad news at length came that this favorite young master was killed, amid all the agony of grief no heart felt the great sorrow more sincerely than hers.

Another and still another of these noble youths fell after deeds of heroic valor, their graves the battlefield, a place of burial fit for men so brave. Only one—the youngest— was brought home to find a resting-place beside the graves of his ancestors.

The old man, their father, his mind

shattered by grief, continued day after day, for several years, to sit in the vine-covered porch, gazing wistfully out, imagining sometimes that he saw in the distance the manly forms of his sons, returning home, mounted on their favorite horses, in the gray uniforms worn the day they went off.

Then he, too, followed, where the "din of war, the clash of arms," is heard no more.

To recall these scenes so blinds my eyes with tears that I cannot write of them. Some griefs leave the heart dumb. They have no language and are given no language, because no other heart could understand, nor could they be alleviated if shared.

CHAPTER IX.

It will have been observed from these reminiscences that the mistress of a Virginia plantation was more conspicuous, although not more important, than the master. In the house she was the mainspring, and to her came all the hundred or three hundred negroes with their various wants and constant applications for medicine and every conceivable requirement.

Attending to these, with directing her household affairs and entertaining company, occupied busily every moment of her life. While all these devolved upon her, it sometimes seemed to me that the master had nothing to do but ride around his estate on the most delightful horse, receive reports from overseers, see that his pack of hounds was fed, and order " repairs about the mill " —the mill seemed always needing repairs!

This view of the subject, however, being entirely from a feminine standpoint, may have been wholly erroneous; for doubtless his mind was burdened with financial matters too weighty to be grasped and comprehended by our sex.

Nevertheless, the mistress held complete sway in her own domain; and that this fact was recognized will be shown by the following incident:

A gentleman, a clever and successful lawyer, one day discovering a negro boy in some mischief about his house, and determining forthwith to chastise him, took him into the yard for that purpose. Breaking a small switch, and in the act of coming down with it upon the boy, he asked: "Do you know, sir, who is master on my place?"

"Yas, sah!" quickly replied the boy. "Miss Charlotte, sah!"

Throwing aside the switch, the gentleman ran into the house, laughed a half hour, and thus ended his only experiment at interfering in his wife's domain.

His wife, "Miss Charlotte," as the negroes called her, was gentle and indulgent to a fault, which made the incident more amusing.

It may appear singular, yet it is true, that

our women, although having sufficient self-possession at home, and accustomed there to command on a large scale, became painfully timid if ever they found themselves in a promiscuous or public assemblage, shrinking from everything like publicity.

Still, these women, to whom a whole plantation looked up for guidance and instruction, could not fail to feel a certain consciousness of superiority, which, although never displayed or asserted in manner, became a part of themselves. They were distinguishable everywhere—for what reason, exactly, I have never been able to find out, for their manners were too quiet to attract attention. Yet a captain on a Mississippi steamboat said to me: "I always know a Virginia lady as soon as she steps on my boat."

"How do you know?" I asked, supposing he would say: "By their plain style of dress and antiquated breastpins."

Said he: "I've been running a boat from Cincinnati to New Orleans for twenty-five years, and often have three hundred passengers from various parts of the world. But if there is a Virginia lady among them, I find it out in half an hour. They take things quietly, and don't complain. Do you see that English lady over there? Well, she has been complaining all the way up the Mississippi River. Nobody can please her. The cabin-maid and steward are worn out with trying to please her. She says it is because the mosquitoes bit her so badly coming through Louisiana. But we are almost at Cincinnati now, haven't seen a mosquito for a week, and she is still complaining!

"Then," he continued, "the Virginia ladies look as if they could not push about for themselves, and for this reason I always feel like giving them more attention than the other passengers."

"We are inexperienced travelers," I replied.

And these remarks of the captain convinced me—I had thought it before—that Virginia women should never undertake to travel, but content themselves with staying at home. However, such restriction would have been unfair unless they had felt like the Parisian who, when asked why the Parisians never traveled, replied: "Because all the world comes to Paris!"

Indeed, a Virginian had an opportunity for seeing much choice society at home; for our watering-places attracted the best people from other States, who often visited us at our houses.

On the Mississippi boat to which I have alluded it was remarked that the negro servants paid the Southerners more constant and deferential attention than the passengers from the non-slaveholding States, although some of the latter were very agreeable and intelligent, and conversed with the negroes on terms of easy familiarity,— showing, what I had often observed, that the negro respects and admires those who make a "social distinction" more than those who make none.

CHAPTER X.

WE were surprised to find in an "Ode to the South," by Mr. M. F. Tupper, the following stanza:

> "Yes, it is slander to say you oppressed them:
> Does a man squander the prize of his pelf?
> Was it not often that he who possessed them
> Rather was owned by his servants himself?"

This was true, but that it was known in the outside world we thought impossible, when all the newspaper and book accounts represented us as miserable sinners for whom there was no hope here or hereafter, and called upon all nations, Christian and civilized, to revile, persecute, and exterminate us. Such representations, however, differed so widely from the facts around us that when we heard them they failed to produce a very serious impression, occasioning often only a smile, with the exclamation: "How little those people know about us!"

We had not the vanity to think that the European nations cared or thought about us, and if the Americans believed these accounts, they defamed the memory of one held up by them as a model of Christian virtue—George Washington, a Virginia slave-owner, whose kindness to his "people," as he called his slaves, entitled him to as much honor as did his deeds of prowess.

But to return to the two last lines of the stanza:

> "Was it not often that he who possessed them
> Rather was owned by his servants himself?"

I am reminded of some who were actually held in such bondage; especially an old gentleman who, together with his whole plantation, was literally possessed by his slaves.

This gentleman [*] was a widower, and no lady presided over his house.

His figure was of medium height and very corpulent. His features were regular and handsome, his eyes were soft brown, almost black, and his hair was slightly gray.

[*] William M. Radford, of Greenfield, Botetourt County.

The expression of his countenance was so full of goodness and sympathy that a stranger meeting him in the road might have been convinced at a glance of his kindness and generosity.

He was never very particular about his dress, yet never appeared shabby.

Although a graduate in law at the university, an ample fortune made it unnecessary for him to practice his profession. Still his taste for literature made him a constant reader, and his conversation was instructive and agreeable.

His house was old and rambling, and— I was going to say his servants kept the keys, but I remember there were *no keys* about the establishment. Even the front door had no lock upon it. Everybody retired at night in perfect confidence, however, that everything was secure enough, and it seemed not important to lock the doors.

The negro servants who managed the house were very efficient, excelling especially in the culinary department, and serving up dinners which were marvels.

The superabundance on the place enabled

them not only to furnish their master's table with the choicest meats, vegetables, cakes, pastries, etc., but also to supply themselves bountifully, and to spread in their own cabins sumptuous feasts, and wedding and party suppers rich enough for a queen.

To this their master did not object, for he told them "if they would supply his table always with an abundance of the best bread, meats, cream, and butter, he cared not what became of the rest."

Upon this principle the plantation was conducted. The well-filled barns, the stores of bacon, lard, flour, etc., literally belonged to the negroes, who allowed their master a certain share!

Doubtless they entertained the sentiment of a negro boy who, on being reproved by his master for having stolen and eaten a turkey, replied: "Well, massa, you see, you got less turkey, but you got dat much more niggah!"

While we were once visiting at this plantation, the master of the house described to us a dairy just completed on a new plan, which for some weeks had been such a hobby with him that he had actually purchased a lock for it, saying he would keep the key himself—which he never did—and have the fresh mutton always put there.

"Come," said he, as he finished describing it, "let us go down and look at it. Bring me the key," he said to a small African, who soon brought it, and we proceeded to the dairy.

Turning the key in the door, the old gentleman said: "Now see what a fine piece of mutton I have here!"

But on entering and looking around, no mutton was to be seen, and instead thereof were buckets of custard, cream, and blancmange. The old gentleman, greatly disconcerted, called to one of the servants: "Florinda! Where is my mutton that I had put here this morning?"

Florinda replied: "Nancy took it out, sah, an' put it in de ole spring house. She say dat was cool enough place for mutton. An' she gwine have a big party to-night, an' want her jelly an' custards to keep cool!"

At this the old gentleman was rapidly becoming provoked, when we laughed so much at Nancy's "cool" proceeding that his usual good nature was restored.

"WHERE IS MY MUTTON?"—*Page* 98.

On another occasion we were one evening sitting with this gentleman in his front porch when a poor woman from the neighboring village came in the yard, and, stopping before the door, said to him:

"Mr. Radford, I came to tell you that my cow you gave me has died."

"What did you say, my good woman?" asked Mr. Radford, who was quite deaf.

The woman repeated in a louder voice: "The cow you gave me has died. And she died because I didn't have anything to feed her with."

Turning to us, his countenance full of compassion, he said: "I ought to have thought about that, and should have sent the food for her cow." Then, speaking to the woman: "Well, my good woman, I will give you another cow to-morrow, and send you plenty of provision for her." And the following day he fulfilled his promise.

Another incident occurs to me, showing the generous heart of this truly good man. One day on the Virginia and Tennessee train, observing a gentleman and lady in much trouble, he ventured to inquire of them the cause, and was informed that they had lost all their money and their railroad tickets at the last station.

He asked the gentleman where he lived, and on what side he was during the war.

"I am from Georgia," replied the gentleman, "and was, of course, with the South."

"Well," said Mr. Radford, pulling from his capacious pocket a large purse, which he handed the gentleman, "help yourself, sir, and take as much as will be necessary to carry you home."

The astonished stranger thanked him sincerely, and handed him his card, saying: "I will return the money as soon as I reach home."

Returned to his own home, and relating the incidents of his trip, Mr. Radford mentioned this, when one of his nephews laughed and said: "Well, uncle, we Virginia people are so easily imposed upon! You don't think that man will ever return your money, do you?"

"My dear," replied his uncle, looking at him reproachfully and sinking his voice, "I was fully repaid by the change which came over the man's countenance."

BEFORE THE WAR.

It is due to the Georgian to add that on reaching home he returned the money with a letter of thanks.

. . . . .

In sight of the hospitable home of Mr. Radford was another, equally attractive, owned by his brother-in-law, Mr. Bowyer. These places had the same name, Greenfield, the property having descended to two sisters, the wives of these gentlemen. They might have been called twin establishments, as one was almost a facsimile of the other. At both were found the same hospitality, the same polished floors, the same style of loaf-bread and velvet rolls, the only difference between the two being that Mr. Bowyer kept his doors locked at night, observed more system, and kept his buggies and carriages in better repair.

These gentlemen were also perfectly congenial. Both had graduated in law, read the same books, were members of the same church, knew the same people, liked and disliked the same people, held the same political opinions, enjoyed the same old Scotch songs, repeated the same old English poetry, smoked the same kind of tobacco, in the same kind of pipes, abhorred alike intoxicating drinks, and deplored the increase of bar-rooms and drunkenness in our land.

For forty years they passed together a part of every day or evening, smoking and talking over the same events and people. It was a picture to see them at night over a blazing wood fire, their faces bright with good nature; and a treat to hear all their reminiscences of people and events long past. With what circumstantiality could they recall old law cases, and describe old duels, old political animosities and excitements! What merry laughs they sometimes had!

Everything on one of these plantations seemed to belong equally to the other. If the ice gave out at one place, the servants went to the other for it as a matter of course; or if the buggies or carriage were out of order at Mr. Radford's, which was often the case, the driver would go over for Mr. Bowyer's without even mentioning the circumstance, and so with everything. The families lived thus harmoniously with never the least interruption for forty years.

Now and then the old gentlemen enjoyed a practical joke on each other, and on one occasion Mr. Radford succeeded so effectually in quizzing Mr. Bowyer that whenever he thought of it afterward he fell into a dangerous fit of laughter.

It happened that a man who had married a distant connection of the Greenfield family concluded to take his wife, children, and servants to pass the summer there, dividing the time between the two houses. The manners, character, and political proclivities of this visitor became so disagreeable to the old gentlemen that they determined he should not repeat his visit, although they liked his wife. One day Mr. Bowyer received a letter signed by this objectionable individual—it had really been written by Mr. Radford— informing Mr. Bowyer that, as one of the children was sick, and the physician advised country air, he would be there the following Thursday with his whole family, to stay some months.

" The impudent fellow!" exclaimed Mr. Bowyer as soon as he read the letter. " He knows how Radford and myself detest him! Still I am sorry for his wife. But I will not be dragooned and outgeneraled by that contemptible fellow. No! I will leave home to-day!"

Going to the back door, he called in a loud voice for his coachman, and ordered his carriage. "I am going" said he, "to Grove Hill for a week, and from there to Lexington, with my whole family, and don't know when I shall be at home again. It is very inconvenient," said he to his wife, "but I must leave home."

Hurrying up the carriage and the family, they were soon off on their unexpected trip.

They stayed at Grove Hill, seven miles off, a week, during which time Mr. Bowyer every morning mounted his horse and rode timidly around the outskirts of his own plantation, peeping over the hills at his house, but afraid to venture nearer, feeling assured it was occupied by the obnoxious visitor. He would not even make inquiries of his negroes whom he met, as to the state and condition of things in his house.

Concluding to pursue his journey to Lexington, and halfway there, he met a young nephew of Mr. Radford's who happened to know all about the quiz, and, immediately suspecting the reason of Mr. Bowyer's exile from home, inquired where he was going, how long he had been from home, etc. Soon guessing the truth, and thinking the joke had been carried far enough, he told the old gentleman he need not travel any further, for it was all a quiz of his uncle's, and there was no one at his house. Thereupon Mr. Bowyer, greatly relieved, turned back and went his way home rejoicing, but "determined to pay Radford," he said, for such a practical joke, which had exiled him from home and given him such trouble. This caused many a good laugh whenever it was told throughout the neighborhood.

The two estates of which I am writing were well named—Greenfield; for the fields and meadows were of the freshest green, and, with majestic hills around, the fine cattle and horses grazing upon them, formed a noble landscape.

This land had descended in the same family since the Indian camp-fires ceased to burn there, and the same forests were still untouched where once stood the Indians' wigwams.

In this connection I am reminded of a tradition in the Greenfield family which showed the heroism of a Virginia boy:

The first white proprietor of this place, the great-grandfather of the present owners, had also a large estate in Montgomery County, called Smithfield, where his family lived, and where was a fort for the protection of the whites when attacked by the Indians.

Once, while the owner was at his Greenfield place, the Indians surrounded Smithfield, and the white women and children took refuge in the fort, while the men prepared for battle. They wanted the proprietor of Smithfield to help them fight and to take command, for he was a brave man; but they could not spare a man to carry him the news. So they concluded to send one of his young sons, a lad thirteen years old, who did not hesitate, but, mounting a fleet horse, set off after dark and rode all night through dense forests filled with hostile Indians, reaching Greenfield, a distance of forty miles, next morning. He soon returned with his father, and the Indians were repulsed. And I always thought that boy was courageous enough for his name to live in history.*

The Indians afterward told how, the whole day before the fight, several of their chiefs had been concealed near the Smithfield house under a large haystack, upon which the white children had been sliding and playing all day, little suspecting the gleaming tomahawks and savage men beneath.

From the Greenfield estate in Botetourt and the one adjacent went the ancestors of the Prestons and Breckinridges, who made these names distinguished in South Carolina and Kentucky. And on this place are the graves of the first Breckinridges who arrived in this country.

All who visited at the homesteads just described retained ever after a recollection of the perfectly cooked meats, bread, etc., seen upon the tables at both houses, there being at each place five or six negro cooks who had been taught by their mistresses the highest style of the culinary art.

During the summer season several of these cooks were hired at the different watering-places, where they acquired great

*John Preston, afterward Governor of Virginia.

fame and made for themselves a considerable sum of money by selling recipes.

A lady of the Greenfield family, who married and went to Georgia, told me she had often tried to make velvet rolls like those she had been accustomed to see at her own home, but never succeeded. Her mother and aunt, who had taught these cooks, having died many years before, she had to apply to the negroes for information on such subjects, and they, she said, would never show her the right way to make them. Finally, while visiting at a house in Georgia, this lady was surprised to see velvet rolls exactly like those at her home.

"Where did you get the recipe?" she soon asked the lady of the house, who replied: "I bought it from old Aunt Rose, a colored cook, at the Virginia Springs, and paid her five dollars."

"One of our own cooks, and my mother's recipe," exclaimed the other, "and I had to come all the way to Georgia to get it, for Aunt Rose never would show me exactly how to make them!"

CHAPTER XI.

Not far from Greenfield was a place called Rustic Lodge.*

This house, surrounded by a forest of grand old oaks, was not large or handsome. But its inmates were ladies and gentlemen of the old English style.

The grandmother, Mrs. Burwell, about ninety years of age, had in her youth been one of the belles at the Williamsburg court in old colonial days. A daughter of Sir Dudley Digges, and descended from English nobility, she had been accustomed to the best society. Her manners and conversation were dignified and attractive.

Among reminiscences of colonial times she remembered Lord Botetourt, of whom she related interesting incidents.

The son of this old lady, about sixty years of age, and the proprietor of the estate, was a true picture of the old English gentle-

* Colonel Burwell's.

man. His manners, conversation, thread-cambric shirt-frills, cuffs, and long queue tied with a black ribbon, made the picture complete. His two daughters, young ladies of refinement, had been brought up by their aunt and grandmother to observe strictly all the proprieties of life.

This establishment was proverbial for its order and method, the most systematic rules being in force everywhere. The meals were served punctually at the same instant every day. Old Aunt Nelly always dressed and undressed her mistress at the same hour. The cook's gentle "tapping at the chamber door" called the mistress to an interview with that functionary at the same moment every morning,—an interview which, lasting half an hour, and never being repeated during the day, resulted in the choicest dinners, breakfasts, and suppers.

Exactly at the same hour every morning the old gentleman's horse was saddled, and he entered the neighboring village so promptly as to enable some of the inhabitants to set their clocks by him.

This family had possessed great wealth in eastern Virginia during the colonial government, under which many of its members held high offices.

But impoverished by high living, entertaining company, and a heavy British debt, they had been reduced in their possessions to about fifty negroes, with only money enough to purchase this plantation, upon which they had retired from the gay and charming society of Williamsburg. They carried with them, however, some remains of their former grandeur: old silver, old jewelry, old books, old and well-trained servants, and an old English coach which was the curiosity of all other vehicular curiosities. How the family ever climbed into it, or got out of it, and how the driver ever reached the dizzy height upon which he sat, was the mystery of my childhood.

But, although egg-shaped and suspended in mid-air, this coach had doubtless, in its day, been one of considerable renown, drawn by four horses, with footman, postilion, and driver in English livery.

How sad must have been its reflections on finding itself shorn of these respectable surroundings, and, after the Revolution, drawn by two republican horses, with footman and driver dressed in republican jeans!

A great-uncle of this family, unlike the coach, never would become republicanized; and his obstinate loyalty to the English crown, with his devotion to everything English, gained for him the title "English Louis," by which name he is spoken of in the family to this day. An old lady told me not long ago that she remembered, when a child, the arrival of "English Louis" at Rustic one night, and his conversation as they sat around the fire,—how he deplored a republican form of government, and the misfortunes which would result from it, saying: "All may go smoothly for about seventy years, when civil war will set in. First it will be about these negro slaves we have around us, and after that it will be something else." And how true "English Louis'" prediction has proven.*

Doubtless this gentleman was avoided and proscribed on account of his English procliv-

* On the route to Rustic was a small village called Liberty, approaching which, and hearing the name, "English Louis" swore he would not pass through any such —— little republican town, and, turning his horses, traveled many miles out of his way to avoid it.

ities. For at that day the spirit of republicanism and hatred to England ran high; so that an old gentleman—one of our relatives whom I well remember—actually took from his parlor walls his coat-of-arms, which had been brought by his grandfather from England, and, carrying it out in his yard, built a fire, and, collecting his children around it to see it burn, said: "Thus let everything English perish!"

Should I say what I think of this proceeding I would not be considered, perhaps, a true republican patriot.

. . . . .

I must add a few words to my previous mention of Smithfield, in Montgomery County, the county which flows with healing waters.

Smithfield, like Greenfield, is owned by the descendants of the first white family who settled there after the Indians, and its verdant pastures, noble forests, and mountain streams and springs, form a prospect wondrously beautiful.

This splendid estate descended to three brothers of the Preston family, who equally divided it, the eldest keeping the homestead, and the others building attractive homes on their separate plantations.

The old homestead was quite antique in appearance. Inside, the high mantelpieces reaching nearly to the ceiling, which was also high, and the high wainscoting, together with the old furniture, made a picture of the olden time.

When I first visited this place, the old grandmother, then eighty years of age, was living. She, like the old lady at Rustic, had been a belle in eastern Virginia in her youth. When she married the owner of Smithfield sixty years before, she made the bridal jaunt from Norfolk to this place on horseback, two hundred miles. Still exceedingly intelligent and interesting, she entertained us with various incidents of her early life, and wished to hear all the old songs which she had then heard and sung herself.

"When I was married," said she, "and first came to Smithfield, my husband's sisters met me in the porch, and were shocked at my pale and delicate appearance. One of them, whispering to her brother, asked: 'Why did you bring that ghost up here?'

And now," continued the old lady, " I have outlived all who were in the house that day, and all my own and my husband's family."

This was certainly an evidence of the health-restoring properties of the water and climate in this region.

The houses of these three brothers were filled with company winter and summer, making within themselves a delightful society. The visitors at one house were equally visitors at the others, and the succession of dinner and evening parties from one to the other made it difficult for a visitor to decide at whose particular house he was staying.

One of these brothers, Colonel Robert Preston, had married a lovely lady from South Carolina, whose perfection of character and disposition endeared her to everyone who knew her. Everybody loved her at sight, and the better she was known the more she was beloved. Her warm heart was ever full of other people's troubles or joys, never thinking of herself. In her house many an invalid was cheered by her tender care, and many a drooping heart revived by her bright Christian spirit. She never omitted an opportunity of pointing the way to heaven; and although surrounded by all the allurements which gay society and wealth could bring, she did not swerve an instant from the quiet path along which she directed others. In the midst of bright and happy surroundings her thoughts and hopes were constantly centered upon the life above; and her conversation—which was the reflex of her heart—reverted ever to this theme, which she made attractive to old and young.

The eldest of the three brothers was William Ballard Preston, once Secretary of the Navy in the cabinet of President Taylor.

CHAPTER XII.

IN the region of country just described and in the counties beyond abound the finest mineral springs, one or more being found on every plantation. At one place there were seven different springs, and the servants had a habit of asking the guests and family whether they would have—before breakfast—a glass of White Sulphur, Yellow Sulphur, Black Sulphur, Alleghany, Alum, or Limestone water!

The old Greenbrier White Sulphur Springs was a favorite place of resort for eastern Virginians and South Carolinians at a very early date, when it was accessible only by private conveyances, and all who passed the summer there went in private carriages. In this way certain old Virginia and South Carolina families met every season, and these old people told us that society there was never so good after the railroads and stages brought "all sorts of people, from all sorts of places." This, of course, we knew nothing about from experience, and it sounded rather egotistical in the old people to say so, but that is what they said.

Indeed, these "old folks" talked so much about what "used to be in their day" at the old White Sulphur, that I found it hard to convince myself that I had not been bodily present, seeing with my own eyes certain knee-buckled old gentlemen, with long queues, and certain Virginia and South Carolina belles attired in short-waisted, simple, white cambrics, who passed the summers there. These white cambrics, we were told, had been carried in minute trunks behind the carriages; and were considered, with a few jewels, and a long black or white lace veil thrown over the head and shoulders, a complete outfit for the reigning belles! Another curiosity was that these white cambric dresses — our grandmothers told us — required very little "doing up:" one such having been worn by Mrs. General Washington — so her granddaughter told me — a whole week without requiring washing! It must have been an age of remarkable women and remarkable cambrics! How little they dreamed then of an era when Saratoga trunks would be indispensable to ladies of much smaller means than Virginia and South Carolina belles!

To reach these counties flowing with mineral waters, the families from eastern Virginia and from South Carolina passed through a beautiful region of Virginia known as Piedmont, and those who had kinsfolk or acquaintances there usually stopped to pay them a visit. Consequently the Piedmont Virginians were generally too busy entertaining summer guests to visit the Springs themselves. Indeed, why should they? No more salubrious climate could be found than their own, and no scenery more grand and beautiful. But it was necessary for the tidewater Virginians to leave their homes every summer on account of chills and fevers.

In the lovely Piedmont region, over which the "Peaks of Otter" rear their giant heads, and chains of blue mountains extend as far as eye can reach, were scattered many pleasant and picturesque homes. And in this section my grandfather bought a plantation, when the ancestral estates in the eastern part of the State had been sold to repay the

British debt, which estates, homesteads, and tombstones with their quaint inscriptions, are described in Bishop Meade's "Old Churches and Families of Virginia."

While the tide-water Virginians were already practicing all the arts and wiles known to the highest English civilization; sending their sons to be educated in England, and receiving therefrom brocaded silks and powdered wigs; and dancing the minuet at the Williamsburg balls with the families of the noblemen sent over to govern the colony,—Piedmont was still a dense forest, the abode of Indians and wild animals.

It was not strange, then, that the Piedmont Virginians never arrived at the opulent manner of living adopted by those on the James and York rivers, who, tradition tells us, went to such excess in high living as to have "hams boiled in champagne," and of whom other amusing and interesting tales have been handed down to us. Although the latter were in advance of the Piedmont Virginians in wealth and social advantages, they were not superior to them in honor, virtue, kindness, or hospitality.

It has been remarked that, "when natural

scenery is picturesque, there is in the human character something to correspond; impressions made on the retina are really made on the soul, and the mind becomes what it contemplates."

The same author continues: "A man is not only *like* what he sees, but he *is* what he sees. The noble old Highlander has mountains in his soul, whose towering peaks point heavenward; and lakes in his bosom, whose glassy surfaces reflect the skies; and foaming cataracts in his heart to beautify the mountain side and irrigate the vale; and evergreen firs and mountain pines that show life and verdure even under winter skies!"

"On the other hand," he writes, "the wandering nomad has a desert in his heart; its dead level reflects heat and hate; a sullen, barren plain,—no goodness, no beauty, no dancing wave of joy, no gushing rivulet of love, no verdant hope. And it is an interesting fact that those who live in countries where natural scenery inspires the soul, and where the necessities of life bind to a permanent home, are always patriotic and high-minded; and those who dwell in the desert are always pusillanimous and groveling!"

If what this author writes be true, and the character of the Piedmont Virginians accords with the scenery around them, how their hearts must be filled with gentleness and charity inspired by the landscape which stretches far and fades in softness against the sky! How must their minds be filled with noble aspirations suggested by the everlasting mountains! How their souls must be filled with thoughts of heaven as they look upon the glorious sunsets bathing the mountains in rose-colored light, with the towering peaks ever pointing heavenward and seeming to say: " Behold the glory of a world beyond!" *

Beneath the shadow of the " Peaks " were many happy homes and true hearts, and, among these, memory recalls none more vividly than Otterburn and its inmates.

Otterburn was the residence of a gentleman and his wife who, having no chil-

* From this vicinity went nine ministers who were eminent in their several churches : two Episcopal bishops, one Methodist bishop, three distinguished Presbyterian and three Baptist divines of talent and fame.

dren, devoted themselves to making their home attractive to visitors, in which they succeeded so well that they were rarely without company, for all who went once to see them went again and again.

This gentleman, Benjamin Donald, was a man of high character,—his accomplishments, manner and appearance marking him "rare," —"one in a century." Above his fellow-men in greatness of soul, he could comprehend nothing mean. His stature was tall and erect; his features bold; his countenance open and impressive; his mind vigorous and cultivated; his bearing dignified, but not haughty; his manners simple and attractive; his conversation so agreeable and enlivening that the dullest company became animated as soon as he came into the room. Truth and lofty character were so unmistakably stamped upon him that a day's acquaintance convinced one he could be trusted forever. Brought up in Scotland, the home of his ancestors, in him were blended the best points of Scotch and Virginia character, —strict integrity and whole-souled generosity and hospitality.

How many days and nights we passed at

his house, and in childhood and youth how many hours were we entertained by his bright and instructive conversation! Especially delightful was it to hear his stories of Scotland, which brought vividly before us pictures of its lakes and mountains and castles. How often did we listen to his account of the wedding-tour to Scotland, when he carried his Virginia bride to the old home at Greenock! And how often we laughed about the Scotch children, his nieces and nephews, who, on first seeing his wife, clapped their hands and shouted: "Oh, mother! are you not glad uncle did not marry a black woman?" Hearing he was to marry a Virginian, they expected to see a savage Indian or negro! And some of the family who went to Liverpool to meet them, and were looking through spy-glasses when the vessel arrived, said they were "sure the Virginia lady had not come, because they saw no one among the passengers dressed in a red shawl and gaudy bonnet like an Indian"!

From this we thought that Europeans must be very ignorant of our country and its inhabitants, and we have since learned that their children are purposely kept ignorant of facts in regard to America and its people.

Among many other recollections of this dear old friend of Otterburn I shall never forget a dream he told us one night, which so impressed us that, before his death, we asked him to write it out, which he did; and, as the copy is before me in his own handwriting, I will insert it here:

"About the time I became of age I returned to Virginia for the purpose of looking after and settling my father's estate. Three years thereafter I received a letter from my only sister, informing me that she was going to be married, and pressing me in the most urgent manner to return to Scotland to be present at her marriage, and to attend to the drawing of the marriage contract. The letter gave me a good deal of trouble, as it did not suit me to leave Virginia at that time. I went to bed one night, thinking much on this subject, but soon fell asleep, and dreamed that I landed in Greenock in the night-time, and pushed for home, thinking I would take my aunt and sister by surprise.

"When I arrived at the door, I found all still and quiet, and the out-door locked. I thought, however, that I had in my pocket my check-key, with which I quietly opened the door and groped my way into the sitting-room, but, finding no one there, I concluded they had gone to bed. I then went upstairs to their bedroom, and found that unoccupied. I then concluded they had taken possession of my bedroom in my absence, but, not finding them there, became very uneasy about them. Then it struck me they might be in the guest's chamber, a room downstairs kept exclusively for company. Upon going there I found the door partially open; I saw my aunt removing the burning coals from the top of the grate preparatory to going to bed. My sister was sitting up in bed, and as I entered the room she fixed her eyes upon me, but did not seem to recognize me. I approached toward her, and, in the effort to make myself known, awoke and found it all a dream. At breakfast next morning I felt wearied and sick, and could not eat, and told the family of my (dream) journey overnight.

"I immediately commenced preparing,

and in a very short time returned to Scotland. I saw my sister married, and she and her husband set off on their 'marriage jaunt.' About a month thereafter they returned, and at dinner I commenced telling them of my dream; but, observing they had quit eating and were staring at me, I laughed, and asked what was the matter, whereupon my brother-in-law very seriously asked me to go on. When I finished, they asked me if I remembered the exact time of my dream. I told them it distressed and impressed me so strongly that I noted it down at the time. I pulled out my pocketbook and showed them the date, ' 14th day of May,' written in pencil. They all rose from the table and took me into the bedroom and showed me, written with pencil on the white mantelpiece, ' 14th of May.'

"I asked them what that meant, and was informed that on that very night—and *the only night* they ever occupied that room during my absence—my aunt was taking the coals off of the fire, when my sister screamed out: 'Brother has come!'

"My aunt scolded her, and said she was dreaming; but she said she had not been to sleep, was sitting up in bed, and *saw me* enter the room, and run out when she screamed. So confident was she that she had seen me, and that I had gone off and hidden, that the whole house was thoroughly searched for me, and as soon as day dawned a messenger was sent to inquire if any vessel had arrived from America, or if I had been seen by any of my friends."

No one who visited Otterburn can forget the smiling faces of the negro servants about the house, who received the guests with as true cordiality as did their mistress, expressing their pleasure by widespread mouths showing white teeth (very white by contrast with their jet-black skin), and when the guests were going away always insisted on their remaining longer.

One of these negro women was not only an efficient servant, but a valuable friend to her mistress.

In the absence of her master and mistress she kept the keys, often entertaining their friends, who, in passing from distant plantations, were accustomed to stop, and who received from her a cordial welcome, finding on the table as many delicacies as if the family had been at home.

No more sincere attachment could have existed than that between this lady and her servant. At last, when the latter was seized with a contagious fever which ended her life, she could not have had a more faithful friend and nurse than was her mistress.

The same fever attacked all the negroes on the plantation, and none can describe the anxiety, care, and distress of their owners, who watched by their beds day and night, administering medicine and relieving the sick and dying.

CHAPTER XIII.

Among other early recollections is a visit with my mother to the plantation of a favorite cousin, not far from Richmond, and one of the handsomest seats on the James River. This residence—Howard's Neck*—was a favorite resort for people from Richmond and the adjacent counties, and, like many others on the river, always full of guests; a round of visiting and dinner parties being kept up from one house to another, so that the ladies presiding over these establishments had no time to attend to domestic duties, which were left to their housekeepers while they were employed entertaining visitors.

The negroes on these estates appeared lively and happy—that is, if singing and laughing indicate happiness; for they went to their work in the fields singing, and returned in the evening singing, after which

* Dr. Cunningham's.

they often spent the whole night visiting from one plantation to another, or dancing until day to the music of the banjo or "fiddle." These dances were wild and boisterous, their evolutions being like those of the savage dances described by travelers in Africa. Although the most perfect timists, their music, with its wild, melancholy cadence, half savage, half civilized, cannot be imitated or described. Many a midnight were we wakened by their wild choruses, sung as they returned from a frolic or "corn-shucking," sounding at first like some hideous, savage yell, but dying away on the air, echoing a cadence melancholy and indescribable, with a peculiar pathos, and yet without melody or sweetness.

Corn-shuckings were occasions of great hilarity and good eating. The negroes from various plantations assembled at night around a huge pile of corn. Selecting one of their number—usually the most original and amusing, and possessed of the loudest voice—they called him "captain." The captain seated himself on top of the pile—a large lightwood torch burning in front of him, and, while he shucked, improvised words and music to a wild " recitative," the chorus of which was caught up by the army of shuckers around. The glare of the torches on the black faces, with the wild music and impromptu words, made a scene curious even to us who were so accustomed to it.

After the corn was shucked they assembled around a table laden with roasted pigs, mutton, beef, hams, cakes, pies, coffee, and other substantials—many participating in the supper who had not in the work. The laughing and merriment continued until one or two o'clock in the morning.

. . . . .

On these James River plantations distinguished foreigners were often entertained, who, visiting Richmond, desired to see something of Virginia country life. Mr. Thackeray was once a guest at one of these places, but Dickens never visited them. Could he have passed a month at any one of the homes I have described, he would, I am sure, have written something more flattering of Americans and American life than is found in "Martin Chuzzlewit" and "American Notes." However, with these we should not quarrel, as some of the sketches, especially the one on "tobacco-chewers," we can recognize.

Every nation has a right to its prejudices —certainly the English people have such a right as regards America, this country appearing to the English eye like a huge mushroom, the growth of a night, and unsubstantial. But it is surely wrong to censure a whole nation—as some have done the Southern people—for the faults of a few. Although the right of a nation to its prejudices be admitted, no one has a right, without thorough examination and acquaintance with the subject, to publish as facts the exaggerated accounts of another nation, put forth by its enemies. The world in this way receives very erroneous impressions.

For instance, we have no right to suppose the Germans a cruel race because of the following paragraph clipped from a recent newspaper:

"The cruelty of German officers is a matter of notoriety, but an officer in an artillery regiment has lately gone beyond precedent in ingenuity of cruelty. Some of his men being insubordinate, he punished them by means of a 'spurring process,' which consisted in jabbing spurs persistently and brutally into their legs. By this process his men were so severely injured that they had to go to the hospital."

Neither have we a right to pronounce all Pennsylvanians cruel to their "helps," as they call them, because a Pennsylvania lady told me "the only way she could manage her help"—a white girl fourteen years old—"was by holding her head under the pump and pumping water upon it until she lost her breath,"—a process I could not have conceived, and which filled me with horror.

But sorrow and oppression, we suppose, may be found in some form in every clime, and in every phase of existence some hearts are "weary and heavy laden." Even Dickens, whose mind naturally sought and fed upon the comic, saw wrong and oppression in the "humane institutions" of his own land!

And Macaulay gives a painful picture of Mme. D'Arblay's life as waiting-maid to Queen Charlotte—from which we are not to infer, however, that all queens are cruel to their waiting-maids.

Mme. D'Arblay—whose maiden name was Frances Burney—was the first female novelist in England who deserved and received the applause of her countrymen. The most eminent men of London paid homage to her genius. Johnson, Burke, Windham, Gibbon, Reynolds, Sheridan, were her friends and ardent eulogists. In the midst of her literary fame, surrounded by congenial friends, herself a star in this select and brilliant coterie, she was offered the place of waiting-maid in the palace. She accepted the position, and bade farewell to all congenial friends and pursuits. "And now began," says Macaulay, "a slavery of five years—of five years taken from the best part of her life, and wasted in menial drudgery. The history of an ordinary day was this: Miss Burney had to rise and dress herself early, that she might be ready to answer the royal bell, which rang at half after seven. Till about eight she attended in the queen's dressing-room, and had the honor of lacing her august mistress's stays, and of putting on the hoop, gown, and neck-handkerchief. The morning was chiefly spent in rummaging drawers and laying fine clothes in their proper places. Then the queen was to be powdered and dressed for the day. Twice a week her Majesty's hair had to be curled and craped; and this operation added a full hour to the business of the toilet. It was generally three before Miss Burney was at liberty. At five she had to attend her colleague, Mme. Schwellenberg, a hateful old toadeater, as illiterate as a chambermaid, proud, rude, peevish, unable to bear solitude, unable to conduct herself with common decency in society. With this delightful associate Frances Burney had to dine and pass the evening. The pair generally remained together from five to eleven, and often had no other company the whole time. Between eleven and twelve the bell rang again. Miss Burney had to pass a half hour undressing the queen, and was then at liberty to retire.

"Now and then, indeed, events occurred which disturbed the wretched monotony of Frances Burney's life. The court moved from Kew to Windsor, and from Windsor back to Kew.

"A more important occurrence was the king's visit to Oxford. Then Miss Burney had the honor of entering Oxford in the last of a long string of carriages, which formed the royal procession, of walking after the queen all day through refectories and chapels, and of standing half dead with fatigue and hunger, while her august mistress was seated at an excellent cold collation. At Magdalen College Frances was left for a moment in a parlor, where she sank down on a chair. A good-natured equerry saw that she was exhausted, and shared with her some apricots and bread, which he had wisely put in his pockets. At that moment the door opened, the queen entered, the wearied attendants sprang up, the bread and fruit were hastily concealed.

"After this the king became very ill, and during more than two years after his recovery Frances dragged on a miserable existence at the palace. Mme. Schwellenberg became more and more insolent and intolerable, and now the health of poor Frances began to give way: and all who saw her pale face, her emaciated figure, and her feeble walk predicted that her sufferings would soon be over.

"The queen seems to have been utterly regardless of the *comfort*, the *health*, the *life*, of her attendants, Weak, feverish, hardly able to stand, Frances had still to rise before seven, in order to dress the sweet queen, and sit up till midnight, in order to undress the sweet queen. The indisposition of the handmaid could not and *did not escape the notice of* her royal mistress. But the *established doctrine of the court was that all sickness* was to be *considered as a pretense until it proved fatal.* The only way in which the invalid could clear herself from the suspicion of malingering, as it is called in the army, was to go on lacing and unlacing, *till she fell down dead at the royal feet.*"

Finally Miss Burney's father pays her a visit in this palace prison, when "she told him that she was miserable; that she was worn with attendance and want of sleep; that she had no comfort in life,—nothing to love, nothing to hope; that her family and friends were to her as though they were not, and were remembered by her as men remember the dead. From daybreak to midnight the same killing labor, the same recreation, more hateful than labor itself, followed each other without variety, without any interval of liberty or repose."

Her father's veneration for royalty amounting to idolatry, he could not bear to remove her from the court—" and, between the dear father and the sweet queen, there seemed to be little doubt that some day or other Frances *would drop down a corpse.* Six months had elapsed since the interview between the parent and the daughter. The resignation was not sent in. The sufferer grew worse and worse. She took bark, but it failed to produce a beneficial effect. She was stimulated with wine; she was soothed with opium, but in vain. Her breath began to fail. The whisper that she was in a decline spread through the court. The pains in her side became so severe that she was forced to crawl from the card-table of the old fury, Mme. Schwellenberg, to whom she was tethered, three or four times in an evening, for the purpose of taking hartshorn. Had she been a negro slave, a humane planter would have excused her from work. But her Majesty showed no mercy. Thrice a day the accursed bell still rang; the queen was still to be dressed for the morning at seven, and to be dressed for the day at noon, and to be undressed at midnight."

At last Miss Burney's father was moved to compassion and allowed her to write a letter of resignation. "Still I could not," writes Miss Burney in her diary, "summon courage to present my memorial from seeing the queen's entire freedom from such an expectation. For though I was frequently so ill in her presence that I could hardly stand, I saw she concluded me, while life remained, inevitably hers.

"At last, with a trembling hand, the paper was delivered. Then came the storm. Mme. Schwellenberg raved like a maniac. The resignation was not accepted. The father's fears were aroused, and he declared, in a letter meant to be shown to the queen, that his daughter must retire. The Schwellenberg raged like a wildcat. A scene almost horrible ensued.

"The queen then promised that, after the next birthday, Miss Burney should be set at liberty. But the promise was ill kept; and her Majesty showed displeasure at being reminded of it."

At length, however, the prison door was

opened, and Frances was free once more. Her health was restored by traveling, and she returned to London in health and spirits. Macaulay tells us that she went to visit the palace, "her *old dungeon, and found her successor already far on the way to the grave, and kept to strict duty, from morning till midnight, with a sprained ankle and a nervous fever.*"

An ignorant and unlettered woman would doubtless not have found this life in the palace tedious, and our sympathy would not have been aroused for her; for as long as the earth lasts there must be human beings fitted for every station, and it is supposed, till the end of all things, there must be cooks, housemaids, and dining-room servants, which will make it never possible for the whole human family to stand entirely upon the same platform socially and intellectually. And Miss Burney's wretchedness, which calls forth our sympathy, was not because she had to perform the duties of waiting-maid, but because to a gifted and educated woman these duties were uncongenial; and congeniality means *happiness;* uncongeniality, *unhappiness.*

CHAPTER XIV.

From the sorrows of Miss Burney in the palace—a striking contrast with the menials described in our own country homes—I will turn to another charming place on the James River—Powhatan Seat, a mile below Richmond, which had descended in the Mayo family two hundred years.

Here, it was said, the Indian chief Powhatan had lived, and here was shown the veritable stone supposed to have been the one upon which Captain Smith's head was laid, when the Indian princess Pocahontas rescued him.

This historic stone, near the parlor window, was only an ugly, dark, broad, flat stone, but imagination pictured ever around it the Indian group, Smith's head upon it, the infuriated chief with uplifted club in the act of dealing the death-blow, the grief and shriek of Pocahontas as she threw herself upon Smith, imploring her father to spare him,—a piercing cry to have penetrated the heart of the savage chief!

Looking out from the parlor window and imagining this savage scene, how strange a contrast met the eye within! Around the fireside assembled the loveliest family group, where kindness and affection beamed in every eye, and father, mother, brothers, and sisters were linked together by tenderest devotion and sympathy.

If natural scenery reflects itself upon the heart, no wonder a "holy calm" rested upon this family, for far down the river the prospect was peace and tranquillity; and many an evening in the summer-house on the river bank we drank in the beauty of soft blue skies, green isles, and white sails floating in the distance.

Many in Richmond remember the delightful weddings and parties at Powhatan Seat, where assembled the *élite* from Richmond, with an innumerable throng of cousins, aunts, and uncles from Orange and Culpeper counties.

On these occasions the house was illuminated by wax lights issuing from bouquets of magnolia leaves placed around the walls near the ceiling, and looking prettier than any glass chandelier.

We, from a distance, generally stayed a week after the wedding, becoming, as it were, a part of the family circle; and the bride did not rush off on a tour as is the fashion nowadays, but remained quietly at home, enjoying the society of her family and friends.

One feature I have omitted in describing our weddings and parties—invariably a part of the picture—was the sea of black faces surrounding the doors and windows to look on the dancing, hear the music, and afterward get a good share of the supper.

Tourists often went to walk around the beautiful grounds at Powhatan—so neatly kept with sea-shells around the flowers, and pleasant seats under the lindens and magnolias—and to see the historic stone; but I often thought they knew not what was missed in not knowing, as we did, the lovely family within.

But, for us, those rare, beautiful days at Powhatan are gone forever; for since the war the property has passed into strange

BEFORE THE WAR. 145

hands, and the family who once owned it will own it no more.

During the late war heavy guns were placed in the family burying-ground on this plantation—a point commanding the river; and here was interred the child of a distinguished general* in the Northern army—a Virginian, formerly in the United States army—who had married a member of the Powhatan family. He was expected to make an attack upon Richmond, and over his child's grave was placed a gun to fire upon him. Such are the unnatural incidents of civil war.

About two miles from Powhatan Seat was another beautiful old place—Mount Erin—the plantation formerly of a family all of whom, except two sisters, had died. The estate, becoming involved, had to be sold, which so grieved and distressed these sisters that they passed hours weeping if accidentally the name of their old home was mentioned in their presence.

Once when we were at Powhatan, and these ladies were among the guests, a member of the Powhatan family ordered the carriage, and took my sister and myself to

* General Scott.

Mount Erin, telling us to keep it a secret when we returned, for "the sisters," said she, "would neither eat nor sleep if reminded of their old home."

A pleasant drive brought us to Mount Erin, and when we saw the box hedges, gravel walks, and linden trees we were no longer surprised at the grief of the sisters whose hearts entwined around their old home. The house was in charge of an old negro woman—the purchaser not having moved in—who showed us over the grounds; and every shrub and flower seemed to speak of days gone by. Even the ivy on the old bricks looked gloomy, as if mourning the light, mirth, and song departed from the house forever; and the walks gave back a deadened echo, as if they wished not to be disturbed by stranger tread. All seemed in a reverie, dreaming a long sweet dream of the past, and entering into the grief of the sisters, who lived afterward for many years in a pleasant home on a pleasant street in Richmond, with warm friends to serve them, yet their tears never ceased to flow at the mention of Mount Erin.

. . . . .

One more plantation picture, and enough will have been described to show the character of the homes and people on our plantations.

The last place visited by my sister and myself before the war of 1861 was Elkwood, a fine estate in Culpeper County, four miles from the railroad station, the residence of Richard Cunningham.

It was the last of June. The country was a scene of enchantment as the carriage rolled us through dark, cool forests, green meadows, fields of waving grain; out of the forests into acres of broad-leaved corn; across pebble-bottomed streams, and along the margin of the Rapidan, which flowed at the base of the hill leading up to the house.

The house was square and white, and the blinds green as the grass lawn and trees in the yard. Inside the house the polished "dry-rubbed" floors, clean and cool, refreshed one on entering like a glass of iced lemonade on a midsummer's day. The old-fashioned furniture against the walls looked as if it thought too much of itself to be set about promiscuously over the floor, like modern fauteuils and divans.

About everything was an air of dignity and repose corresponding with the manners and appearance of the proprietors, who were called "Uncle Dick" and "Aunt Jenny"—the *a* in "Aunt" pronounced very broad.

Aunt Jenny and Uncle Dick had no children, but took care of numerous nieces and nephews, kept their house filled to overflowing with friends, relatives, and strangers, and were revered and beloved by all. They had no pleasure so great as taking care of other people. They lived for other people, and made everybody comfortable and happy around them. From the time Uncle Dick had prayers in the morning until family prayers at bedtime they were busy bestowing some kindness.

Uncle Dick's character and manners were of a type so high that one felt elevated in his presence; and a desire to reach his standard animated those who knew him. His precept and example were such that all who followed them might arrive at the highest perfection of Christian character.

Uncle Dick had requested Aunt Jenny, when they were married, forty years before, to have on his table every day dinner enough for six more persons than were already in the house, "in case," he said, "he should meet friends or acquaintances, while riding over his plantation or in the neighborhood, whom he wished to ask home with him to dinner." This having been always a rule, Aunt Jenny never sat at her table without dinner enough for six more,—and hers were no commonplace dinners; no hasty-puddings, no saleratus bread, no soda cakes, no frozen-starch ice-cream, no modern shorthand recipes, but genuine old Virginia cooking. And all who want to know what that was can find out all about it in Aunt Jenny's book of copied recipes—if it is extant—or in that of Mrs. Harrison, of Brandon. But as neither of these books may ever be known to the public, their "sum and substance" may be given in a few words:

"Have no shams. Procure an abundance of the freshest, richest *real* cream, milk, eggs, butter, lard, best old Madeira wine, all the way from Madeira, and never use a particle of soda or saleratus about anything or under any pressure."

These were the ingredients Aunt Jenny

used, for Uncle Dick had rare old wine in his cellar which he had brought from Europe thirty years before, and every day was a feast-day at Elkwood. And the wedding breakfasts Aunt Jenny used to get up when one of her nieces married at her house—as they sometimes did—were beyond description.

While at Elkwood, observing every day that the carriage went to the depot empty and returned empty, we inquired the reason, and were informed that Uncle Dick, ever since the cars had been passing near his plantation, ordered his coachman to have the carriage every day at the station, " in case some of his friends might be on the train, and might like to stop and see him"!

Another hospitable rule in Uncle Dick's house was that company must never be kept waiting in his parlor, and so anxious was his young niece to meet his approbation in this as in every particular that she had a habit of dressing herself carefully, arranging her hair beautifully—it was in the days, too, when smooth hair was fashionable— before lying down for the afternoon siesta, "in case," she said, "someone might call, and Uncle Dick had a horror of visitors waiting." This process of reposing in a fresh muslin dress and fashionably arranged hair required a particular and uncomfortable position, which she seemed not to mind, but dozed in the most precise manner without rumpling her hair or her dress.

Elkwood was a favorite place of resort for Episcopal ministers, whom Aunt Jenny and Uncle Dick loved to entertain. And here we met the Rev. Philip Slaughter, the learned divine, eloquent preacher, and charming companion. He had just returned from a visit to England, where he had been entertained in palaces. Telling us the incidents of his visit, "I was much embarrassed at first," said he, "at the thought of attending a dinner-party given in a palace to me, a simple Virginian, but, on being announced at the drawing-room door and entering the company, I felt at once at ease, for they were all ladies and gentlemen, such as I had known at home—polite, pleasant, and without pretense."

This gentleman's conversational powers were not only bright and delightful, but also the means of turning many to righteousness—for religion was one of his chief themes.

A proof of his genius and eloquence was given in the beautiful poem recited—without ever having been written—at the centennial anniversary of old Christ Church in Alexandria. This was the church in which General Washington and his family had worshiped, and around it clustered many memories. Mr. Slaughter, with several others, had been invited to make an address on the occasion, and one night, while thinking about it, an exquisite poem passed through his mind, picturing scene after scene in the old church—General Washington, with his head bowed in silent prayer; infants at the baptismal font; young men and maidens in bridal array at the altar; and funeral trains passing through the open gate.

On the night of the celebration, when his turn came, finding the hour too late and the audience too sleepy for his prose address, he suddenly determined to "dash off" the poem, every word of which came back to him, although he had never written it. The audience roused up electrified, and, as the recitation proceeded, their enthusiasm reached the highest pitch. Never had there been such a sensation in the old church before. And, next morning, the house at which he was stopping was besieged by reporters begging "copies" and offering good prices, but the poem remains unwritten to this day.

Elkwood, like many other old homes, was burned by the Northern army in 1862, and not a tree or flower remains to mark the spot that for so many years was the abode of hospitality and good cheer.

In connection with Culpeper County, it is due here to state that it excelled all others in ancient and dilapidated buggies and carriages, seeming to be a regular infirmary for all the disabled vehicles of the Old Dominion. Here their age and infirmities received every care and consideration, being propped up, tied up, and bandaged up in every conceivable manner; and, strangest of all, rarely depositing their occupants in the road, which was prevented by cautious old gentlemen riding alongside, who, watching for and discovering the weakest points, stopped and securely tied up fractured parts with bits of twine, rope, or chain always carried in buggy- or carriage-boxes for that purpose. These surgical operations, although not ornamental, strengthened and sustained these venerable vehicles, and produced a miraculous longevity.

Many more sketches might be given of pleasant country homes—themes worthy a better pen than mine; for Brandon, Westover, Shirley, Carter Hall, Lauderdale, Vaucluse, and others, linger in the memory of hundreds who once knew and loved them—especially Vaucluse, which, although far removed from railroads, stage-coaches, and public conveyances, was overflowing with company throughout the year. For the Vaucluse girls were so bright, so fascinating, and so bewitchingly pretty, that they attracted a concourse of visitors, and were sure to be belles wherever they went.

And many remember the owner of Vaucluse, Mr. Blair Dabney, that pure-hearted Christian and cultivated gentleman who, late in life, devoted himself to the Episcopal ministry, and labored faithfully in the Master's cause, preaching in country churches, "without money and without price." Surely his reward is in heaven.

Besides these well-ordered establishments, there were some others owned by inactive men, who smoked their pipes, read their books, left everything very much to the management of their negroes, and seemed content to let things tumble down around them.

One of these places we used to call "Topsy-Turvy Castle," and another "Haphazard."

At such places the negro quarters—instead of being neat rows of white cabins in the rear of the house, as on other plantations—occupied a conspicuous place near the front, and consisted of a solid, long, ugly brick structure, with swarms of negroes around the windows and doors, appearing to have nothing in the world to do and never to have done anything.

Everything had a "shackling," lazy appearance. The master was always, it appeared to us, reading a newspaper in the front porch, and never observing anything that was going on. The house was so full of idle negroes standing about the halls and stairways that one could scarcely make one's way up or down stairs. Everything needed repair, from the bed upon which you slept to the family coach which took you to church.

Few of the chairs had all their rounds and legs, and, when completely disabled, were sent to the garret, where they accumulated in great numbers, and remained until pressing necessity induced the master to raise his eyes from his paper long enough to order "Dick" to "take the four-horse wagon and carry the chairs to be mended."

A multitude of kinsfolk and acquaintance usually congregated here. And at one place, in order to accommodate so many, there were four beds in a chamber. These high bedsteads presented a remarkable appearance,—the head of one going into the side of another, the foot of one into the head of another, and so on, looking as if they had never been "placed," but as if their curious juxtaposition had been the result of an earthquake.

One of these houses is said to have been greatly improved in appearance during the war by the passage of a cannon-ball through the upper story, where a window had been needed for many years.

BEFORE THE WAR.

But the owners of these places were so genuinely good, one could not complain of them, even for such carelessness. For everybody was welcome to everything. You might stop the plows if you wanted a horse, or take the carriage and drive for a week's journey, and, in short, impose upon these good people in every conceivable way.

Yet, in spite of this topsy-turvy management—a strange fact connected with such places—they invariably had good light-bread, good mutton, and the usual abundance on their tables.

We suppose it must have been a recollection of such plantations which induced the negro to exclaim, on hearing another sing "Ole Virginny Nubber Tire": "Umph! ole Virginny nubber tire, kase she nubber done nuthin' fur to furtigue herself!"

CHAPTER XV.

CONFINING these reminiscences strictly to plantation life, no mention has been made of the families we knew and visited in some of our cities, whose kindness to their slaves was unmistakable, and who, owning only a small number, could better afford to indulge them.

At one of these houses this indulgence was such that the white family were very much under the control of their servants.

The owner of this house, Charles Mosby, an eminent lawyer, was a man of taste and learning, whose legal ability attracted many admirers, and whose refinement, culture, and generous nature won enthusiastic friends.

Although considered the owner of his house, it was a mistake, if ownership means the right to govern one's own property; for beyond his law-papers, library, and the privilege of paying all the bills, this gentleman had no "rights" there whatever, his house, kitchen, and premises being under the entire command of "Aunt Fanny," the cook, a huge mulatto woman, whose word was law, and whose voice thundered abuse if any dared to disobey her.

The master, mistress, family, and visitors all stood in awe of Aunt Fanny, and yet could not do without her, for she made unapproachable light-bread and conducted the affairs of the place with distinguished ability.

Her own house was in the yard, and had been built especially for her convenience. Her furniture was polished mahogany, and she kept most delicious preserves, pickles, and sweetmeats of her own manufacture, with which to regale her friends and favorites. As we came under that head, we were often treated when we went in to see her after her day's work was over, or on Sundays.

Although she "raved and stormed" considerably—which she told us she was "obliged to do, honey, to keep things straight"—she had the tenderest regard for her master and mistress, and often said: "If it warn't for *me*, they'd have nuthin' in the world, and things here would go to destruction."

So Aunt Fanny "kept up this family," as she said, for many years, and many amusing incidents might be related of her.

On one occasion her master, after a long and exciting political contest, was elected to the legislature. Before all the precincts had been heard from, believing himself defeated, he retired to rest, and, being naturally feeble, was quite worn out. But at midnight a great cry arose at his gate, where a multitude assembled, screaming and hurrahing. At first he was uncertain whether they were friends to congratulate him on his victory or the opposite party to hang him, as they had threatened, for voting an appropriation to the Danville Railroad. It soon appeared they had come to congratulate him, when great excitement prevailed, loud cheers, and cries for a speech. The doors were opened and the crowd rushed in. The hero soon appeared and delivered one of his graceful and satisfactory speeches.

Still the crowd remained cheering and storming about the house, until Aunt Fanny, who had made her appearance in

"AUNT FANNY 'SPERSED DAT CROWD.'"—*Page 16.*

full dress, considering the excitement had been kept up long enough, and that the master's health was too delicate for any further demonstration, determined to disperse them. Rising to her full height, waving her hand, and speaking majestically, she said: "Gentlemen, Mars' Charles is a feeble pusson, an' it's time for him to take his res'. He's been kep' 'wake long enough now, an' it's time for me to close up dese doors!"

With this the crowd dispersed, and Aunt Fanny remained mistress of the situation, declaring that if she "hadn't come forward an' 'spersed dat crowd, Mars' Charles would have been a dead man befo' mornin'."

Aunt Fanny kept herself liberally supplied with pocket-money, one of her chief sources of revenue being soap, which she made in large quantities and sold at high prices; especially what she called her "butter soap," which was in great demand, and which was made from all the butter which she did not consider fresh enough for the delicate appetites of her mistress and master. She appropriated one of the largest basement rooms, had it shelved, and filled it with soap. In order to carry on business so extensively, huge logs were kept blazing on the kitchen hearth under the soap-pot day and night. During the war, wood becoming scarce and expensive, "Mars' Charles" found that it drained his purse to keep the kitchen fire supplied.

Thinking the matter over one day in his library, and concluding it would greatly lessen his expenses if Aunt Fanny could be prevailed upon to discontinue her soap trade, he sent for her, and said very mildly:

"Fanny, I have a proposition to make you."

"What is it, Mars' Charles?"

"Well, Fanny, as my expenses are very heavy now, if you will give up your soap-boiling for this year, I will agree to pay you fifty dollars."

With arms akimbo, and looking at him with astonishment but with firmness in her eye, she replied: "Couldn't possibly do it, Mars' Charles; because *soap*, sir, *soap's my main-tain-ance!*"

With this she strode majestically out of the room. "Mars' Charles" said no more, but continued paying fabulous sums for wood, while Aunt Fanny continued boiling her soap.

This woman not only ordered but kept all the family supplies, her mistress having no disposition to keep the keys or in any way interfere with her.

But at last her giant strength gave way, and she sickened and died. Having no children, she left her property to one of her fellow-servants.

Several days before her death we were sitting with her mistress and master in a room overlooking her house. Her room was crowded with negroes who had come to perform their religious rites around the deathbed. Joining hands, they performed a savage dance, shouting wildly around her bed. This was horrible to hear and see, especially as in this family every effort had been made to instruct their negro dependents in the truths of religion; and one member of the family, who spent the greater part of her life in prayer, had for years prayed for Aunt Fanny and tried to instruct her in the true faith. But although an intelligent woman, she seemed to cling to the superstitions of her race.

After the savage dance and rites were over, and while we sat talking about it, a gentleman—the friend and minister of the family—came in. We described to him what we had just witnessed, and he deplored it bitterly with us, saying he had read and prayed with Aunt Fanny and tried to make her see the truth in Jesus. He then marked some passages in the Bible, and asked me to go and read them to her. I went, and said to her: "Aunt Fanny, here are some verses Mr. Mitchell has marked for me to read to you, and he hopes you will pray to the Saviour as he taught you." Then said I: "We are afraid the noise and dancing have made you worse."

Speaking feebly, she replied: "Honey, dat kind o' 'ligion suit us black folks better 'en yo' kind. What suit Mars' Charles' mind karn't suit mine."

And thus died the most intelligent of her race—one who had been surrounded by pious persons who had been praying for her and endeavoring to instruct her. She had also enjoyed through life not only the comforts but many of the luxuries of earth, and when she died her mistress and master lost a sincere friend.

CHAPTER XVI.

This chapter will show how "Virginia beat biscuit" procured for a man a home and friends in Paris.

One morning in the spring of 185—, a singular-looking man presented himself at our house. He was short of stature, and enveloped in furs, although the weather was not cold. Everything about him which could be gold, was gold, and so we called him "the gold-tipped man." He called for my mother, and when she went into the parlor, he said to her:

"Madam, I have been stopping several weeks at the hotel in the town of L., where I met a boy—Robert—who tells me he belongs to you. As I want such a servant, and he is anxious to travel, I come, at his request, to ask if you will let me buy him and take him to Europe. I will pay any price."

"I could not think of it," she replied.

"I have determined never to sell one of my servants."

"But," continued the man, "he is anxious to go, and has sent me to beg you."

"It is impossible," said she, "for he is a great favorite with us, and the only child his mother has."

Finding her determined, the man took his leave, and went back to the town, twenty-five miles off; but returned next day accompanied by Robert, who entreated his mother and mistress to let him go.

Said my mother to him: "Would you leave your mother and go with a stranger to a foreign land?"

"Yes, madam. I love my mother, an' you an' all de fambly—you always been so good to me—but I want travel, an' dis gent'man say he give me plenty o' money an' treat me good, too."

Still she refused. But the boy's mother, finally yielding to his entreaty, consented, and persuaded her mistress, saying: "If he is willing to leave me, and so anxious to go, I will give him up."

Knowing how distressed we all would be at parting with him, he went off without

BEFORE THE WAR. 167

coming to say "good-by," and wrote his mother from New York what day he would sail with his new master for Europe.

At first his mother received from him presents and letters, telling her he was very much delighted, and "had as much money as he knew what to do with." But after a few months he ceased to write, and we could hear nothing from him.

At length, when eighteen months had elapsed, we were one day astonished to see him return home, dressed in the best Parisian style. We were rejoiced to see him again, and his own joy at getting back cannot be described. He ran over the yard and house, examining everything, and said: "Mistess, I aint see no place pretty as yours, an' no lady look to me like you in all de finest places I bin see in Europ', an' no water tas'e good like de water in our ole well. An' I dream 'bout you all, an' 'bout ev'y ole chur an' table in dis house, an' wonder ef uvver I'd see 'um ag'in."

He then gave us a sketch of his life since the "gold-tipped man" had become his master. Arrived in Paris, his master and himself took lodgings, and a teacher was employed to come every day and instruct Robert in French. His master kept him well supplied with money, never giving him less than fifty dollars at a time. His duties were light, and he had ample time to study and amuse himself.

After enjoying such elegant ease for eight or nine months he awoke one morning and found himself deserted and penniless! His master had absconded in the night, leaving no vestige of himself except a gold dressing-case and a few toilet articles of gold, which were seized by the proprietor of the hotel in payment of his bill.

Poor Robert, without money and without a friend in this great city, knew not where to turn. In vain he wished himself back in his old home.

"If I could only find some Virginian to whom I could appeal," said he to himself. And suddenly it occurred to him that the American Minister, Mr. Mason, was a Virginian. When he remembered this, his heart was cheered, and he lost no time in finding Mr. Mason's house.

Presenting himself before the American Minister, he related his story, which was not at first believed. "For," said Mr. Mason, "there are so many impostors in Paris it is impossible to believe you."

Robert protested he had been a slave in Virginia, had been deserted by his owner in Paris, and begged Mr. Mason to keep him at his house, and take care of him.

Then Mr. M. asked many questions about people and places in Virginia, all of which were accurately answered. Finally he said: "I knew well the Virginia gentleman who was, you say, your master. What was the color of his hair?" This was also satisfactorily answered, and Robert began to hope he was believed, when Mr. Mason continued:

"Now, there is one thing which, if you can do, will convince me you came from Virginia. Go in my kitchen and make me some old Virginia beat biscuit, and I will believe everything you have said!"

"I think I kin, sir," said Robert, and, going into the kitchen, rolled up his sleeves, and set to work.

This was a desperate moment, for he had never made a biscuit in his life, although he had often watched the proceeding as

"Black Mammy," the cook at home, used to beat, roll, and manipulate the dough on her biscuit-box.

"If I only could make them look like hers!" thought he, as he beat, and rolled, and worked, and finally stuck the dough all over with a fork. Then, cutting them out and putting them to bake, he watched them with nervous anxiety until they resembled those he had often placed on the table at home.

Astonished and delighted with his success, he carried them to the American Minister, who exclaimed: "Now I *know* you came from old Virginia!"

Robert was immediately installed in Mr. John Y. Mason's house, where he remained a faithful attendant until Mr. Mason's death, when he returned with the family to America.

Arriving at New York, he thought it impossible to get along by himself, and determined to find his master. For this purpose he employed a policeman, and together they succeeded in recovering "the lost master,"— this being a singular instance of a "slave in pursuit of his fugitive master."

BEFORE THE WAR. 171

The "gold-tipped man" expressed much pleasure at his servant's fidelity, and, handing him a large sum of money, desired him to return to Paris, pay his bill, bring back his gold dressing-box and toilet articles, and, as a reward for his fidelity, take as much money as he wished and travel over the Continent.

Robert obeyed these commands, returned to Paris, paid the bills, traveled over the chief places in Europe, and then came again to New York. Here he was appalled to learn that his master had been arrested for forgery, and imprisoned in Philadelphia. It was ascertained that the forger was an Englishman and connected with an underground forging establishment in Paris. Finding himself about to be detected in Paris, he fled to New York, and, other forgeries having been discovered in Philadelphia, he had been arrested.

Robert lost no time in reporting himself at the prison, and was grieved to find his master in such a place.

Determined to do what he could to relieve the man who had been a good friend to him, he went to a Philadelphia lawyer, and said to him: "Sir, the man who is in prison bought me in Virginia, and has been a kind master to me; I have no money, but if you will do your best to have him acquitted, I will return to the South, sell myself, and send you the money."

"It is a bargain," replied the lawyer. "Send me the money, and I will save your master from the penitentiary."

Robert returned to Baltimore, sold himself to a Jew in that city, and sent the money to the lawyer in Philadelphia. After this he was bought by a distinguished Southern Senator—afterward a general in the Southern army*—with whom he remained, and to whom he rendered valuable services during the war.

. . . . .

Other instances were known of negroes who preferred being sold into slavery rather than take care of themselves. There were some in our immediate neighborhood who, finding themselves emancipated by their master's will, begged the owners of neighboring plantations to buy them, saying they preferred having "white people to take care

* General Robert Toombs.

BEFORE THE WAR.

of them." On the Wheatly plantation, not far from us, there is still living an old negro who sold himself in this way, and cannot be persuaded *now* to accept his freedom. After the war, when all the negroes were freed by the Federal government, and our people were too much impoverished longer to clothe and feed them, this old man refused to leave the plantation, but clung to his cabin, although his wife and family moved off and begged him to accompany them.

" No," said he, " I nuvver will leave dis plantation, an' go off to starve wid free niggers."

Not even when his wife was very sick and dying could he be persuaded to go off and stay one night with her. He had long been too old to work, but his former owners indulged him by giving him his cabin, and taking care of him through all the poverty which has fallen upon our land since the war.

Many of us remember this old man, Harrison Mitchell, who was an unusual character, high-toned and reliable. His father was an Indian and his mother a negress. He resembled the Indian, with straight black hair, brown skin, and high cheek-bones. His great pride was that he had "cum out de Patrick Henry estate an use to run a freight boat wid flour down de Jeemes Ruver fum Lynchbu'g to Richmon' long fo' dar was a sign o' town at Lynch's Ferry." But his great and consuming theme, especially after the war, was the impossibility of the negroes taking care of themselves "bedout no white man," and nothing ever reconciled him to his own freedom. Taking his seat in our back porch, where my mother usually entertained him, we would assemble to hear him talk. I would ask: "Well, Uncle Harrison, what do you think of freedom now after ten years?"

"Lord, mistess, what I t'ink o' freedom? Why, mistess, dese niggers is no mo' kakalate to take kur o' deyselves dan 'possum. An' I tells 'em so. Kase what is a nigger bedout white man? He aint nuthin', an' he aint gwine be nuthin' no ways dey fix it. An' dey aint gwine stay free, kase de Lord nuvver 'tends 'um to be nuthin' bedout white folks. Kase ev'ybody know nigger aint got no hade. I nuvver want no nigger be takin' kur o' me. I looks to my white folks to take kur o' me. I 'lonks to Mars' Robert an' aint gwine lef his plantation tell I die. What right Yankees got settin' me free, an' den karn't take kur o' me? No! niggers is niggers, an' gwine be niggers, an' white folks got to take kur on 'em tell end o' screeation. An' der Lord gwine put ev'y single one on 'em back in slavery jes' as sure as you born."

True to his word, old Harrison refused to wear an article of clothing "ef de white folks didn't give it to him." And his daughter, wishing to give him a blanket, asked her former young mistress to let him think it was from *her*, or he would not take it.

At last "Mars' Robert" was on his deathbed. Old Harrison went in to see him for the last time.

"Mars' Robert," said he, "I got one reques' to make fo' you die."

"What is it?" asked his master.

"Mars' Robert, I want to be buried right outside de gate o' de garden lot where you an' Miss Lucy is buried, so I kin see you fus' on de mornin' o' de resurrection."

"Harrison, you shall be buried *inside* the

lot with us," replied "Mars' Robert" distinctly, and a lady who heard it told me she never saw such radiant happiness as the old man's face expressed when these words fell on his ear.

CHAPTER XVII.

O BRIGHT-WINGED peace! long didst thou rest o'er the homes of old Virginia; while cheerful wood fires blazed on hearthstones in parlor and cabin, reflecting contented faces with hearts full of peace and good will toward men! No thought entered there of harm to others; no fear of evil to ourselves. Whatsoever things were honest, whatsoever things were pure, whatsoever things were gentle, whatsoever things were of good report, we were accustomed to hear around these parlor firesides; and often would our grandmothers say:

"Children, ours is a blessed country! There never will be another war! The Indians have long ago been driven out, and it has been nearly a hundred years since the English yoke was broken!"

The history of our country, to our minds, was contained in two pictures on the walls of our house: "The Last Battle with the

Indians," and "The Surrender of Lord Cornwallis at Yorktown."

No enemies within or without our borders, and peace established among us forever! Such was our belief. And we wondered that men should get together and talk their dry politics, seeing that General Washington and Thomas Jefferson—two of our Virginia plantation men—had established a government to last as long as the earth, and which could not be improved. Yet they *would* talk, these politicians, around our parlor fire, where often our patience was exhausted hearing discussions, in which we could not take interest, about the Protective Tariff, the Bankrupt Law, the Distribution of Public Lands, the Resolutions of '98, the Missouri Compromise, and the Monroe Doctrine. These topics seemed to afford them intense pleasure and satisfaction, for, as the "sparks fly upward," the thoughts of men turn to politics.

In 1859 we had a visit from two old friends of our family—a distinguished Southern Senator and the Secretary of War *—both accustomed to swaying multi-

* General Toombs and General Floyd.

tudes by the power of their eloquence—which lost none of its force and charm in our little home circle. We listened with admiration as they discussed the political issues of the day—no longer a subject uninteresting or unintelligible to us, for every word was of vital importance. Their theme was, *The best means of protecting our plantation homes and firesides.* Even the smallest children now comprehended the greatest politicians.

Now came the full flow and tide of Southern eloquence—real soul-inspiring eloquence.

Many possessing this gift were in the habit of visiting us at that time; and all dwelt upon one theme—the secession of Virginia—with glowing words from hearts full of enthusiasm; all agreeing it was better for States, as well as individuals, to separate rather than quarrel or fight.

But there was one *—our oldest and best friend—who differed from these gentlemen; and his eloquence was gentle and effective. Unlike his friends, whose words, earnest and electric, overwhelmed all around, this gentle-

* Charles Mosby.

man's power was in his composure of manner without vehemence. His words were well selected without seeming to have been studied; each sentence was short, but contained a gem, like a solitaire diamond.

For several months this gentleman remained untouched by the fiery eloquence of his friends, like the Hebrew children in the burning furnace. Nothing affected him until one day the President of the United States demanded by telegraph fifty thousand Virginians to join an army against South Carolina. And then this gentleman felt convinced it was not the duty of Virginians to join an army against their friends.

About this time we had some very interesting letters from the Hon. Edward Everett—who had been for several years a friend and agreeable correspondent —giving us his views on the subject, and very soon after this all communication between the North and South ceased, except through the blockade, for four long years.

And then came the long dark days—the days when the sun seemed to shine no more; when the eyes of wives, mothers, and

BEFORE THE WAR.

sisters were heavy with weeping; when men sat up late in the night studying military tactics; when grief-burdened hearts turned to God in prayer.

The intellectual gladiators who had discoursed eloquently of war around our fireside buckled their armor on and went forth to battle.

Band after band of brave-hearted, bright-faced youths from Southern plantation homes came to bleed and die on Virginia soil; and for four long years old Virginia was one great camping-ground, hospital, and battlefield. The roar of cannon and the clash of arms resounded over the land. The groans of the wounded and dying went up from hillside and valley. The hearts of women and children were sad and careworn. But God, to whom we prayed, protected us in our plantation homes, where no white men or even boys remained, all having gone into the army. Only the negro slaves stayed with us, and these were encouraged by our enemies to rise and slay us; but God in his mercy willed otherwise. Although advised to burn our property and incited by the enemy to destroy their former owners, these negro slaves remained faithful, manifesting kindness, and in many instances protecting the white families and plantations during their masters' absence.

Oh! the long terrible nights passed by these helpless women and children, the enemy encamped around them, the clash of swords heard against the doors and windows, the report of guns on the air which might be sending death to their loved ones!

But why try to describe the horrors of such nights? Who that has not experienced them can know how we felt? Who can imagine the heartsickness when, stealing to an upper window at midnight, we watched the fierce flames rising from some neighboring home, expecting our own to be destroyed by the enemy before daylight in the same way?

Such pictures, dark and fearful, were the only ones familiar to us in old Virginia those four dreadful years.

At last the end came—the end which seemed to us saddest of all. But God knoweth best. Though "through fiery trials" he had caused us to pass, he had not forsaken us. For was not his mercy signally shown in the failure of the enemy to incite our negro slaves to insurrection during the war? Through his mercy those who were expected to become our enemies remained our friends. And in our own home, surrounded by the enemy those terrible nights, our only guard was a faithful negro servant who slept in the house, and went out every hour to see if we were in immediate danger; while his mother —the kind old nurse—sat all night in a rocking-chair in our room, ready to help us. Had we not, then, amid all our sorrows, much to be thankful for?

Among such scenes one of the last pictures photographed on my memory was that of a negro boy who was very ill with typhoid fever in a cabin not far off, and who became greatly alarmed when a brisk firing, across our house, commenced between the contending armies. His first impulse—as it always had been in trouble—was to fly to his mistress for protection, and, jumping from his bed, his head bandaged with a white cloth, and looking like one just from the grave, he passed through the firing as fast as he could, screaming: " O mistess, take kur o' me! Put me in yo' closet, and hide me from de Yankees!" He fell at the door exhausted. My mother had him brought in, and a bed was made for him in the library. She nursed him carefully, but he died in a day or two from fright and exhaustion.

Soon after this came the surrender at Appomattox, and negro slavery ended forever.

All was ruin around us,—tobacco factories burned down, sugar and cotton plantations destroyed. The negroes fled from these desolated places, crowded together in wretched shanties on the outskirts of towns and villages, and found themselves, for the first time in their lives, without enough to eat, and with no class of people particularly interested about their food, health, or comfort. Rations were furnished them a short time by the United States government, with promises of money and land which were never fulfilled. Impoverished by the war, it was a relief to us no longer to have the responsibility of supporting them. This would, indeed, have been impossible in our starving condition.

Years have passed, and the old homes have been long deserted where the scenes I have attempted to describe were enacted. The heads of the families lie buried in the old graveyards, while their descendants are scattered from the Atlantic to the Pacific, always holding sacred in memory the dear old homes in Virginia.

The descendants of the negroes here portrayed,—where are they? It would take a long chapter, indeed, to tell of them. Many are crowded on the outskirts of the towns and villages North and South, in wretched thriftlessness and squalor, yet content and without ambition to alter their condition.

On the other hand, a good proportion of the race seek to improve their opportunities in schools and colleges, provided partly by the aid of Northern friends, but principally from taxes paid by their former owners in spite of the impoverished condition of the South.

Many have acquired independent homes, with the laudable purpose of becoming useful and respected citizens. The majority, however, are best pleased with itinerancy.

It is needless to say that those of the latter class can never become desirable domestics in a well-ordered, cleanly house.

And those whose youth has been passed in schoolrooms, with no training in the habits of refined life, have not acquired sufficient education to avail much in the line of letters. Thus the problem of their race remains unsolved, even by those who know it most intimately.

In the matter of classical education the question occurs: Will the literature of the one race meet the requirements of the other, or the heroes and heroines of one be acceptable to the other? Has not God given each country its distinct race and literature? The history of every country occupied by antagonistic races has been that the stronger has dominated or exterminated the other.

Thinking of the superficial education at some of our schools, I am reminded of a colored boy's subject for a composition.

Not long since a " colored scholar," seventeen years old, with very fair intelligence, who had never missed a day at the public school, was asked by a white gentleman who was much interested in the boy, and who often took the trouble to explain to him words in common use, the meaning of which the boy was wholly ignorant,—

BEFORE THE WAR.

"Peter, what lessons have you to-night?"

"Well, sir, I got a composition to write to-night."

"A composition? What's your subject?"

"Dey tell me, sir, to write a composition on de administration o' Mr. Pierce."

"Administration of Mr. Pierce!" exclaimed the gentleman, himself an eminent journalist and statesman. "And what could you know about the administration of Mr. Pierce? Did you ever hear of Mr. Pierce?"

"No, sir, I nuvver has."

. . . . .

The tie which once bound the two races together is broken forever, and entire separation in churches and schools prevents mutual interest or intercourse.

Our church schools are doing much to elevate and improve the negroes, and we have to thank many kind, warm friends in the North for timely aid in missionary boxes, books, and Bibles to carry on the colored Sunday-school work in which many Southern people are deeply interested, without the means of conducting them as they wish.

The negroes still have a strange belief in what they call "tricking," and often the most intelligent, when sick, will say they have been "tricked," for which they have a regular treatment and "trick doctors" among themselves. This "tricking" we cannot explain, and only know that when one negro became angry with another he would bury in front of his enemy's cabin door a bottle filled with pieces of snakes, spiders, bits of tadpole, and other curious substances; and the party expecting to be "tricked" would hang up an old horseshoe outside of his door to ward off the "evil spirits."

Since alienated from their former owners they are, as a general thing, more idle and improvident; and, unfortunately, the tendency of their political teaching has been to make them antagonistic to the better class of white people, which renders it difficult for them to be properly instructed. That such animosity should exist toward those who could best understand and help them is to be deplored. For the true negro character cannot be fully comprehended or described but by those who, like ourselves, have always lived with them.

At present their lives are devoted to a religious excitement which demoralizes them, there seeming to be no connection between their religion and morals. In one of their Sabbath schools is a teacher who, although often arrested for stealing, continues to hold a high position in the church.

Their improvidence has passed into a proverb, many being truly objects of charity; and whoever would now write a true tale of poverty and wretchedness may take for the hero "Old Uncle Tom without a cabin." For "Uncle Tom" of the olden time, in his cabin, with a blazing log fire and plenty of corn bread, and the Uncle Tom of to-day, are pictures of very different individuals.

CHAPTER XVIII.

Reviewing these sketches of our early days, I feel that they are incomplete without a tribute to some of the teachers employed to instruct us. Even in colonial days our great-grandfathers had been sent to England to be educated, so that education was considered all-important in our family, especially with my father, who exerted his influence for public schools and advocated teaching the negroes to read and write, contending that this would increase their value as well as their intelligence.

Determining that my sister and myself should have proper educational advantages, he engaged, while we were young children, a most extraordinary woman to teach us—a Danish lady, better versed in many other languages than in our own. Her name was Henriquez, and her masculine appearance, mind, and manners were such as to strike terror into the hearts of youthful pupils. Having attended lectures at a college in Copenhagen with several female friends alike ambitious to receive a scientific education, Mme. Henriquez scorned feminine acquirements and acquaintances, never possessing, to my knowledge, a needle or thimble. Her conversation was largely confined to scientific subjects, and was with men whenever possible, rarely descending to anything in common with her own sex. Sometimes in school our recitations would be interrupted by recollections of her early days in Copenhagen, and, instead of pursuing a lesson in geography or grammar, we would be entertained with some marvelous story about her father's palace, the marble stable for his cows, etc. In the midst of correcting a French or German exercise she would sometimes order a waiter of refreshments to be brought into the schoolroom and placed before her on a small table which had a history, being made, as she often related, from a tree in her father's palace grounds, around which the serfs danced on the day of their emancipation. She had a favorite dog named Odin which was allowed the privilege of the schoolroom, and any girl guilty of disrespect to Odin was in serious disgrace.

This Danish lady was succeeded by one of a wholly different type, all grace and accomplishments, a Virginian, and the widow of Major Lomax of the United States Army.

Mrs. Lomax had several accomplished daughters who assisted in her school, and the harp, piano, and guitar were household instruments. The eldest daughter contributed stories and verses, which were greatly admired, to periodicals of that day. One of these stories, published in a Northern journal, won for her a prize of one hundred dollars, and the school-girls were thrilled to hear that she spent it all for a royal purple velvet gown to wear to Miss Preston's wedding in Montgomery County.

In this school Mrs. Lomax introduced a charming corps of teachers from Boston, most cultivated and refined women, whom it will always be a pleasure to remember. Among these were Mrs. Dana, with her accomplished daughter, Miss Matilda Dana, well known in the literary world then as a writer of finished verses.

We had also a bright, sweet-natured little

Frenchwoman, Mlle. Roget, who taught her native language.

Besides these teachers we had a German gentleman, a finished pianist and linguist; and the recollections of those days are like the delicious music that floated around us then from those master-musicians.

After such pleasant school-days at home we were sent away to a fashionable boarding-school in the city of Richmond, presided over by a lady of great dignity and gentleness of manner, combined with high attainments. She was first Mrs. Otis of Boston, and afterward Mrs. Meade of Virginia.

At her school were collected many interesting teachers and pupils. Among the former were Miss Prescott of Boston and Miss Willis, sister of N. P. Willis, both lovable and attractive.

Among the noted girls at Mrs. Meade's school was Amélie Rives* of Albemarle

* This interesting girl married Mr. Sigourney of Massachusetts, and after the war, as she was crossing the ocean to Europe with her husband and all her children (except one son) the ill-fated ship sank with nearly all on board. We have heard that, as the ship was going down, Amélie, her husband, and her children formed a circle, hand in hand, and were thus buried in the deep.

County, Va. She spoke French fluently, and seemed to know much about Paris and the French court, her father having been Minister to France.

We looked upon Amélie with great admiration, and, as she wrote very pretty poetry, every girl in the school set her heart upon having some original verses in her album, a favor which Amélie never refused.

Closing this chapter on schools suggests the great difference in the objects and methods of a Virginia girl's education then and now. At that period a girl was expected not only to be an ornament to the drawing-room, but to be also equipped for taking charge of an establishment and superintending every detail of domestic employment on a plantation—the weaving, knitting, sewing, etc.—for the comfort of the negro servants to be some day under her care. I have thus seen girls laboriously draw the threads of finest linen, and backstitch miles of stitching on their brothers' collars and shirt-bosoms. Having no brothers to sew for, I looked on in amazement at this dreary task, and I have since often wished that those persevering and devoted women could come back and live their lives over again in the days of sewing-machines.

At that day the parents of a girl would have shuddered at the thought of her venturing for a day's journey without an escort on a railway car, being jostled in a public crowd, or exposed in any way to indiscriminate contact with the outside world, while the proposition of a collegiate course for a woman would have shocked every sensibility of the opposite sex.

How the men of that time would stand aghast to see the girl of the present day elbowing her way through a crowd, buying her ticket at the railway station, interviewing baggage-agents, checking trunks, and seating herself in the train to make a long journey alone, perhaps to enter some strange community and make her living by the practice of law or medicine, lecturing, teaching, telegraphing, newspaper-reporting, typewriting, bookkeeping, or in some other of the various avenues now open to women!

Whether the new system be any improvement upon the old remains open for discussion. It is certain that these widely opposed methods must result in wholly different types of feminine character.

CHAPTER XIX.

THE scenes connected with the late war will recall to the mind of every Southern man and woman the name of Robert E. Lee—a name which will be loved and revered as long as home or fireside remains in old Virginia, and which sets the crowning glory on the list of illustrious men from plantation homes. Admiration and enthusiasm naturally belong to victory, but the man must be rare indeed who in defeat, like General Lee, receives the applause of his countrymen.

It was not alone his valor, his handsome appearance, his commanding presence, his perfect manner, which won the admiration of his fellow-men. There was something above and beyond all these—his true Christian character. Trust in God ennobled his every word and action. Among the grandest of human conquerors was he, for, early enlisting as a soldier of the Cross, to fight against the world, the flesh, and the devil, he fought the " good fight," and the victor's crown awaited him in the " kingdom not made with hands."

Trust in God kept him calm in victory as in defeat. When I remember General Lee during the war, in his family circle at Richmond, then at the height of his renown, his manner, voice, and conversation were the same as when, a year after the surrender, he came to pay my mother a visit from his Lexington home.

His circumstances and surroundings were now changed: no longer the stars and epaulets adorned his manly form; but, dressed in a simple suit of pure white linen, he looked a king, and adversity had wrought no change in his character, manner, or conversation.

To reach our house he made a journey, on his old war horse " Traveler," forty miles across the mountains, describing which, on the night of his arrival, he said:

"To-day an incident occurred which gratified me more than anything that has happened for a long time. As I was riding over the most desolate mountain region, where not even a cabin could be seen, I was surprised to find, on a sudden turn in the road, two little girls playing on a large rock. They were very poorly clad, and after looking a moment at me began to run away. 'Children,' said I, 'don't run away. If you could know *who* I am, you would know that I am the last man in the world for anybody to run from now.'

"'But we do know you,' they replied.

"'You never saw me before,' I said, 'for I never passed along here.'

"'But we do know you,' they said. 'And we've got your picture up yonder in the house, and you are General Lee! And we aint dressed clean enough to see you.'

"With this they scampered off to a poor low hut on the mountain side."

It was gratifying to him to find that even in this lonely mountain hut the children had been taught to know and revere him.

He told us, too, of a man he met the same day in a dense forest, who recognized him, and, throwing up his hat in the air, said: "General, *please* let me cheer you," and fell to cheering with all his lungs!

. . . . .

My last recollections of General Lee,

when making a visit of several weeks at his house the year before his death, although not coming properly under the head of "plantation reminiscences," may not be inappropriate here.

It has been said that a man is never a hero to his valet; but this could not have been said of General Lee, for those most intimately connected with him could not fail to see continually in his bearing and character something above the ordinary level, something of the hero.

At the time of my visit the Commencement exercises of the college of which he was president were going on. His duties were necessarily onerous. Sitting up late at night with the board of visitors, and attending to every detail with his conscientious particularity, there was little time for him to rest. Yet every morning of that busy week he was ready, with his prayer-book under his arm, when the church bell called its members to sunrise service.

It is pleasant to recall all that he said at the breakfast, dinner, and tea table, where in his hospitality he always insisted upon bringing all who chanced to be at his house at

those hours—on business or on social call.*
This habit kept his table filled with guests,
who received from him the most graceful
courtesy.

Only once did I hear him speak regretfully
of the past. It was one night when, sitting
by him on the porch in the moonlight, he
said to me, his thoughts turning to his early
childhood:

"It was not my mother's wish that I
should receive a military education, and I
ought to have taken her advice; for," he
continued very sadly, "my education did
not fit me for this civil life."

In this no one could agree with him, for
it seemed to all that he adorned and satisfactorily filled every position in life, civil or
military.

There was something in his manner
which naturally pleased everyone without his
making an effort; at the same time a dignity and reserve which commanded respect

*Here was seen the Mount Vernon silver, which had descended to Mrs. General Washington's great-grandson, General Custis Lee, and which was marvelously preserved during the war, having been concealed in different places—and once was buried near Lexington in a barn which was occupied by the enemy several days.

and precluded anything like undue familiarity. All desirable qualities seemed united in him to render him popular.

It was wonderful to observe—in the evenings when his parlors were overflowing with people, young and old, from every conceivable place—how by a word, a smile, a shake of the hand, he managed to give *all* pleasure and satisfaction, each going away charmed with him.

The applause of men excited in him no vanity; for those around soon learned that the slightest allusion or compliment, in his presence, to his valor or renown, instead of pleasing, rather offended him. Without vanity, he was equally without selfishness.

One day, observing several quaint articles of furniture about his house, and asking Mrs. Lee where they came from, she told me that an old lady in New York city—of whom neither herself nor the general had ever before heard—concluded to break up housekeeping. Having no family, and not wishing to sell or remove her furniture to a boarding-house, she determined to give it to "the *greatest living man*," and that man was General Lee.

She wrote a letter asking his acceptance of the present, requesting that, if his house was already furnished and he had no room, he would use the articles about his college.

The boxes arrived. But—such was his reluctance at receiving gifts—weeks passed and he neither had them opened nor brought to his house from the express office.

Finally, as their house was quite bare of furniture, Mrs. Lee begged him to allow her to have them opened, and he consented.

First there was among the contents a beautiful carpet large enough for two rooms, at which she was delighted, as they had none. But the general, seeing it, quickly said: "That is the very thing for the floor of the new chapel! It must be put there."

Next were two sofas and a set of chairs. "The very things we want," again exclaimed the general, "for the platform of the new chapel!"

Then they unpacked a sideboard. "This will do *very well*," said the general, "to be placed in the basement of the chapel to hold the college papers!"

And so with everything the lady had sent, only keeping for his own house the articles which could not possibly be used for the college or chapel,—a quaint work-table, an ornamental clock, and some old-fashioned preserve-dishes—although his own house was then bare enough, and the donor had particularly requested that only those articles which they did not need at their home should go to the college.

The recollection of this visit, although reviving many pleasant hours, is very sad, for it was the last time I saw the dear, kind face of Mrs. Lee, of whom the general once said, when one of us, alluding to him, used the word "hero": "My dear, *Mrs.* Lee is the hero. For although deprived of the use of her limbs by suffering, and unable for ten years to walk, I have never heard her murmur or utter one complaint."

And the general spoke truly,—Mrs. Lee was a heroine. With gentleness, kindness, and true feminine delicacy, she had strength of mind and character a man might have envied. Her mind, well stored and cultivated, made her interesting in conversation; and a simple cordiality of manner made her beloved by all who met her.

During this last visit she loved to tell

about her early days at Arlington—her own and her ancestors' plantation home—and in one of these conversations gave me such a beautiful sketch of her mother—Mrs. Custis—that I wish her every word could be remembered that I might write it here.

Mrs. Custis was a woman of saintly piety, her devotion to good works having long been a theme with all in that part of Virginia. She had only one child—Mrs. Lee—and possessed a very large fortune. In early life she felt that God had given her a special mission, which was to take care of and teach the three hundred negroes she had inherited.

"Believing this," said Mrs. Lee to me, "my mother devoted the best years of her life to teaching these negroes, for which purpose she had a school-house built in the yard, and gave her life up to this work; and I think it an evidence of the ingratitude of their race that, although I have long been afflicted, only one of those negroes has written to inquire after me, or offered to nurse me."

These last years of Mrs. Lee's life were passed in much suffering, she being unable to move any part of her body except her hands and head. Yet her time was devoted to working for her church. Her fingers were always busy with fancy-work, painting, or drawing,—she was quite an accomplished artist,—the results of which were sold for the purpose of repairing and beautifying the church in sight of her window, and as much an object of zeal and affection with her as the chapel was with the general.

Indeed, the whole family entered into the general's enthusiasm about this chapel, just then completed, especially his daughter Agnes, with whom I often went there, little thinking it was so soon to be her place of burial.

In a few short years all three—General Lee, his wife and daughter—were laid here to rest, and this chapel they had loved so well became their tomb.

CHAPTER XX.

ALL plantation reminiscences resemble a certain patchwork, made when we were children, of bright pieces joined with black squares. The black squares were not pretty, but if left out the character of the quilt was lost. And so with the black faces—if left out of our home pictures of the past, the character of the picture is destroyed.

What I have written is a simple record of facts in my experience, without an imaginary scene or character; intended for the descendants of those who owned slaves in the South, and who may in future wish to know something of the lofty character and virtues of their ancestors.

The pictures are strictly true; and should it be thought by any that the brightest have alone been selected, I can only say I knew no others.

It would not be possible for any country to be entirely exempt from crime and wickedness, and in Virginia, too, these existed; for prisons, penitentiaries, and courts of justice were here, as elsewhere, necessary; but it is my sincere belief that the majority of Southern people were true and good. And that they have accomplished more than any other nation toward civilizing and elevating the negro race may be shown from the following paragraph in a late magazine:

"From a very early date the French had their establishment on the western coast of Africa. In 1364 their ships visited that portion of the world. But with all this long intercourse with the white man the natives have profited little. Five centuries have not civilized them, so as to be able to build up institutions of their own. Yet the French have always succeeded better than the English with the negro and Indian element."

Civilization and education are slow; for, says a modern writer:

"After the death of Roman intellectual activity, the seventh and eighth centuries were justly called dark. If Christianity was to be one of the factors in producing the present splendid enlightenment, she had no time to lose, and she lost no time. She was the only power at that day that could begin the work of enlightenment. And, starting at the very bottom, she wrought for *nine hundred years* alone. The materials she had to work upon were stubborn and unmalleable. For one must be somewhat civilized to have a taste for knowledge at all; and one must know something to be civilized at all. She had to carry on the double work of civilizing and educating. Her progress was necessarily slow at first. But after some centuries it began to increase in arithmetical progression until the sixteenth century."

Then our ancestors performed a great work—the work allotted them by God, civilizing and elevating an inferior race in the scale of intelligence and comfort. That this race may continue to improve, and finally be the means of carrying the Gospel into their native Africa, should be the prayer of every earnest Christian.

Never again will the negroes find a people so kind and true to them as the Southerners have been.

There is much in our lives not intended for us to comprehend or explain; but, believing that nothing happens by chance, and that our forefathers have done their duty in the place it had pleased God to call them, let us cherish their memory, and remember that the Lord God Omnipotent reigneth.

> " For he who rules each wondrous star,
>   And marks the feeble sparrow's fall,
> Controls the destiny of man,
>   And guides events however small.
>
> " Man's place of birth, his home, his friends,
>   Are planned and fixed by God alone—
> ' Life's lot is cast '—e'en death he sends
>   For some wise purpose of his own."

THE END.